W9-ASG-144

59-65

Frontiers of Science

SECRETS OF
ANIMAL BEHAVIOR

S. T. Butler
and Robert Raymond

FEB 1975
RECEIVED
OHIO DOMINICAN
COLLEGE LIBRARY
COLUMBUS, OHIO
43219

Anchor Books

Anchor Press/Doubleday

Garden City, New York

1975

ISBN: 0–385–09692–5
Library of Congress Catalog Card Number 74–20495
Copyright © 1975 by Science Features / All rights reserved
Printed in the United States of America

93627

FRONTIERS OF SCIENCE books, written and produced by S. T. Butler and Robert Raymond, are available in five volumes from Doubleday. *Introduction to Physics* covers atoms, Einstein, and energy. *Introduction to Modern Medicine* describes progress being made by medical science in its battle to combat and finally control man's two greatest killers—heart disease and cancer. *Introduction to Earth Science* looks at earthquakes, volcanoes, hurricanes, the new ice age, and many other aspects of earth science. *Introduction to Astronomy* discusses the formation of galaxies, the birth of the solar system, the evolution of life on our planet, and the possibilities of its existence on other worlds. *Secrets of Animal Behavior* explores the animal kingdom, examining animal migration, hibernation, survival techniques of bees, chemical warfare by insects, and chimpanzee communication.

156
B986s
1975

Contents . . .

93627

Limits to togetherness

One of the key factors in animal behavior is the maintenanc[e] an individual's territory.

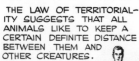

THE NEAT SPACING OF MIGRATING BIRDS RESTING ON TELE—PHONE WIRES . . .

... THE LION SNARLING AT THE LION-TAMER, BUT NOT ATTACKING HIM ...

... THE BULL REFUSING TO MOVE FROM A PARTIC—ULAR SPOT IN THE BULLRING...

...ALL THESE, ACCORD[ING] TO THE FINDINGS OF ANTHROPOLOGY, AR[E] PART OF A BASIC ANIM[AL] LAW OF "TERRITORIALITY["]WHICH GOVERNS ALL ANIMAL GROUPS —— INCLUDING MAN .

THE LAW OF TERRITORIAL—ITY SUGGESTS THAT ALL ANIMALS LIKE TO KEEP A CERTAIN DEFINITE DISTANCE BETWEEN THEM AND OTHER CREATURES.

THEY TEND TO RETREAT IF ANYTHING APPROACHES THIS INVISIBLE LINE —— THE "FLIGHT DISTANCE".

DESPITE THE IMPRESSION OF DANGER, THE ANIMAL WILL USUALLY NOT ATTACK UNLESS AN INTRUDER PENETRATES THIS "PERSONAL" ZONE.

IN WILD ANIMALS, THE SENSE OF TERRITORIALIT[Y] HELPS ENSURE THE SUR[-]VIVAL OF THE SPECIES B[Y] AN INGENIOUS CONTROL MECHANISM . . .

...NIMAL BIOLOGISTS HAVE ...SCOVERED HOW THE LAW ... TERRITORIALITY KEEPS ...OWN ANIMAL COMMUNITIES ... A SIZE SUITED TO ...EIR ENVIROMENT.

EVERY CREATURE HAS ITS PERSONAL TERRITORY. OVERCROWDING CAUSES THIS TO BE INVADED, TRIGGERING AGGRESSION AND TENSION.

FIGHTING AND CONTINUED OVER-STIMULATION OF THE ADRENAL GLANDS LEADS TO EVENTUAL WEAKNESS, AND DISEASE KILLS ENOUGH ANIMALS TO RESTORE THE PACK TO ITS PROPER SIZE.

ONE RODENT, THE SCANDINAVIAN LEMMING, IS EVEN FORCED INTO MASS SUICIDE BY OVERCROWDING, OR LOSS OF TERRITORY.

...OMESTICATED FARM ANIMALS RETAIN ...HE INSTINCT OF TERRITORIALITY; ...HICH IS TIED UP WITH THE ...PECKING ORDER" FOUND ...N ANY MIXED GROUP.

...THOSE AT THE BOTTOM OF THE SOCIAL SCALE ...ONLY AVOID BEING BULLIED BY KEEPING AWAY ...FROM THOSE AT THE TOP.

WHEN INTENSIVE PRODUCTION METHODS FORCE CREATURES CLOSER TOGETHER THAN THEIR "INDIVIDUAL DISTANCE", THEY FIGHT.

AGGRESSION RELEASES ADRENALIN, WHICH CAUSES ANIMALS TO CONSUME ENERGY WHICH WOULD OTHERWISE GO INTO GROWTH, AND THE WEAKER ONES DO NOT SURVIVE.

...HE SENSE OF ...MELL IS A KEY ...ACTOR IN THE ...NIMAL INSTINCT OF ...RRITORIALITY —— ...E DESIRE FOR ...ERSONAL "LIVING ...OOM".

ACCORDING TO SOME ANTHROPOLOGISTS, MAN ALSO RETAINS HIS SENSE OF TERRITORIAL-ITY, AN EVOLUTIONARY TRAIT.

BUT BECAUSE MAN'S SENSE OF SMELL IS NOW RUDIMENTARY, HE CAN LIVE A HIGH-DENSITY URBAN EXISTENCE WITH HIS FELLOW MAN.

EVEN SO, RIOTS IN OVERCROWDED SLUMS MAY INDICATE THAT MAN HIMSELF IS APPROACHING THE LIMIT OF HIS TOLER-ANCE OF "TOGETHERNESS."

5

Mysteries of hibernatio

Some warm-blooded animals have a remarkable ability to sur
for long periods at temperatures close to freezing, which would
other mammals.

SCIENTISTS SEEKING A BETTER UNDERSTANDING OF THE BODY'S MANY SURVIVAL TECHNIQUES OFTEN FIND CLUES IN ANIMAL BEHAVIOR.

BY EFFICIENTLY REGULATING HIS BODY TEMPERATURE, MAN CAN LIVE IN A WIDER RANGE OF CLIMATES THAN MOST OTHER MAMMALS

BUT ONE GROUP OF WARM-BLOODED MAMMALS HAS A CAPABILITY (DENIED TO MAN) OF EXISTING FOR LONG PERIODS WITH A BODY TEMPERATURE CLOSE TO FREEZING.

ZOOLOGISTS TODAY ARE TRYING TO LOCATE AND EXPLAIN THE MECHANIS WHICH MAKES POSSIBLE THE REMARKABLE PROCE OF HIBERNATION.

BY CONTRAST WITH REPTILES AND FISHES, MAMMALS AND BIRDS MAINTAIN. A CONSTANT BODY TEMPERATURE, USUALLY HIGHER THAN THEIR SURROUNDINGS.

"THIS IS ACHIEVED BY CHEMICAL "BURNING" OF FATS; EXCESSIVE HEAT LOSS IS CONTROLLED BY A THERMOREGULATOR IN THE BRAIN.

IN COLD SURROUNDINGS, PROTECTIVE RESPONSES ARE INVOKED: ERECTION OF FUR OR FEATHERS TO IMPROVE INSULATION, SHIVERING TO RAISE HEAT PRODUCTION BY MUSCULAR ACTIVITY.

BUT THE HIBERNATO CAN SOMEHOW TURN DOWN THEIR THERM REGULATORS, BECOM IN EFFECT COLDBLOO AND FOLLOWING TEM ERATURE CHANGES THE AIR....

...SEARCHERS AT THE UNIVERSITY ...TORONTO IN CANADA REPORT ...MARKABLE ASPECTS OF HIBERNATION, ...ICH STILL DEFY EXPLANATION.

THE GROUND SQUIRREL, NORMALLY WARM-BLOODED, SPENDS THE WINTER WITH ITS BODY A FEW DEGREES ABOVE FREEZING; THIS WOULD KILL ORDINARY MAMMALS, INCLUDING MAN.

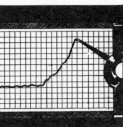

ITS HEART BEATS PERHAPS ONCE PER MINUTE; METABOLIC CYCLES CONTINUE JUST SUFFICIENTLY TO PRE-VENT ACTUAL FREEZING.

HIBERNATION ENDS SUDDENLY, AS IF A SWITCH HAD BEEN THROWN: ITS TEMPE-RATURE RISES RAPIDLY TO NORMAL—— AS MUCH AS 50 DEG. IN THREE HOURS.

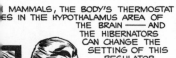

...N MAMMALS, THE BODY'S THERMOSTAT ...ES IN THE HYPOTHALAMUS AREA OF THE BRAIN —— AND THE HIBERNATORS CAN CHANGE THE SETTING OF THIS REGULATOR.

SIGNIFICANTLY, THE HYPOTHALAMUS ALSO CONTAINS THE "APPETITE CENTER", WHICH PREVENTS ANIMALS FROM OVER-EATING.

BEFORE HIBERNATION BEGINS, HOWEVER, ANIMALS EAT HUGELY AND STORE UP FAT —— THE "FUEL" WHICH WILL MAINTAIN THEIR TEMPERATURE JUST ABOVE FREEZING.

THE MECHANISM WHICH INDUCES THE TORPOR OF HIBERNATION MAY THUS BE TRIGGERED WHEN THE ANIMAL REACHES A CERTAIN WEIGHT . . . .

...URPRISINGLY, HIBERNATION IS NOT ...DUCED SOLELY BY THE ONSET ...F WINTER'S SHORTER DAYS ...ND LOWER TEMPERATURES.

SOME ANIMALS WILL HIBERNATE IN ROOMS KEPT ILLUMINATED 24 HOURS A DAY, AT A CONSTANT TEMPERATURE. IS SOME KIND OF BIO-LOGICAL CLOCK INVOLVED?

RESEARCH IN CANADA SUGGESTS RATHER THAT FATNESS STARTS THE CYCLE; IT ENDS WHEN THE FAT IS USED UP, TO A POINT WHICH ENDANGERS THE ANIMAL'S SURVIVAL.

SCIENTISTS ARE NOW SEEKING LINKS WITH THE BRAIN MECHANISM WHICH CAUSES SIMILAR, IF LESSER, FLUCTUATIONS IN WEIGHT, TEMPERATURE, AND ACTIVITY IN NON-HIBERNATORS —— INCLUDING MAN . . . .

Annual biological clock

Besides the biological clocks which control daily cycles activity, some animals appear to have an annual clock which independent of external seasonal changes.

MANY LIVING ORGANISMS HAVE A BUILT-IN "BIOLOGICAL CLOCK" WHICH REGULATES SOME DAILY BODILY CYCLES, INCLUDING TEMPERATURE, KIDNEY FUNCTION, AND DIGESTION.

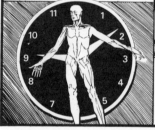

THESE "CIRCADIAN RHYTHMS" AS THEY ARE CALLED, FOLLOW A 24-HOUR PATTERN, ALTHOUGH THEY WORK INDEPENDENTLY OF THE DAILY RISING AND SETTING OF THE SUN.

WHEN THESE RHYTHMS ARE THROWN OUT OF PHASE WITH OUR DAILY LIFE—AS BY JET TRAVEL INTO A DIFFERENT TIME ZONE—THE BODY SUFFERS DISTURBANCE.

IT HAS NOW BEEN DISCOVERED THAT SOM ANIMALS ALSO HAVE A ANNUAL BIOLOGICAL CLOCK, WHICH OPERATE INDEPENDENTLY OF EXTERNAL SEASONAL SIGNALS. . .

THE DISCOVERY OF THE ANNUAL BIOLOGICAL CLOCK IN ANIMALS WAS MADE IN CANADA, ALMOST BY ACCIDENT. . .

DO NOT DISTURB HIBERNATING ANIMALS

. . .ZOOLOGISTS AT TORONTO UNIVERSITY WERE STUDYING THE HIBERNATING HABITS OF A SQUIRREL, KEPT IN A WINDOWLESS ROOM, RECEIVING 12 HOURS ARTIFICIAL LIGHT EACH DAY.

WITH THE ROOM KEPT AT FREEZING POINT, THE SQUIRREL KEPT ACTIVE AND MAINTAINED ITS BODY TEMPERATURE AT A NORMAL 37 DEG. C. FOR SEVERAL MONTHS.

BUT IN AUTUMN (ALTHOUGH IT COULD NOT SEE THE DAYS OUTSIDE SHORTENIN THE SQUIRREL STOPPED EATING, LOWERED ITS BO TEMPERATURE TO 1 DEG. C AND WENT INTO HIBERNATION. . . .

THE SQUIRREL HIBERNATING IN A WHOLLY ARTIFICIAL ENVIRONMENT AT TORONTO UNIVERSITY SUDDENLY WOKE UP IN APRIL, WITH THE COMING OF SPRING OUTSIDE. . .

WITHIN TWO HOURS IT HAD RAISED ITS BODY TEMPERATURE FROM 1 DEG. C. TO NORMAL (37 DEG. C.), AND HAD BEGUN EATING.

STUDIES OVER SEVERAL YEARS PROVED WITHOUT DOUBT THE SQUIRREL'S POSSESSION OF AN INTERNAL "CLOCK" WITH A CYCLE OF ABOUT ONE YEAR. . .

ALTHOUGH DEPRIVED OF ALL SIGNS OF EXTERNAL SEASONAL CHANGES, IT REMAINED ACTIVE UNTIL THE NEXT OCTOBER, WHEN IT AGAIN WENT INTO HIBERNATION.

EVEN MORE CONVINCING PROOF OF THE CANADIAN SQUIRREL'S ANNUAL BIOLOGICAL CLOCK CAME FROM STUDIES OF ANIMALS BORN AND RAISED IN THE LABORATORY.

NEVER HAVING SEEN DAYLIGHT, OR EXPERIENCED OUTSIDE SEASONS, THEY, TOO, HIBERNATED REGULARLY ON SCHEDULE WHEN KEPT IN AN ARTIFICIAL ENVIRONMENT.

THIS PROVES THAT THE "CLOCK" IS SET GENETICALLY, AND NOT "IMPRINTED" BY EXPOSURE TO THE ENVIRONMENT AFTER BIRTH.

EVEN WHEN KEPT IN A ROOM AT BODY TEMPERATURE WHICH PREVENTED THEM FROM HIBERNATING, THE SQUIRRELS ATE LESS AND THUS LOST WEIGHT DURING "WINTER" AND RESUMED FEEDING IN "SPRING".

A BIOLOGICAL ANNUAL "CLOCK" CLEARLY HELPS ANIMALS PREPARE FOR CHANGED SITUATIONS BEFORE THEY ACTUALLY OCCUR.

THE CANADIAN SQUIRREL MUST BEGIN TO LAY DOWN EXTRA BODY FAT BEFORE WINTER ARRIVES —AND OBVIOUSLY RELIES ON ITS "CLOCK".

THE INTRIGUING QUESTION REMAINS: DOES MAN POSSESS AN ANNUAL CLOCK, AS HE UNDOUBTEDLY HAS A DAILY ONE?

THE IMPLICATIONS COULD BE IMPORTANT FOR LONG-DURATION SPACE TRAVEL, WHEN ASTRONAUTS WILL COMPLETELY LACK THE REFERENCES PROVIDED BY NORMAL SEASONAL CHANGES ON EARTH. . .

Survival in the deser

In the most inhospitable habitat on earth, man is at a criti disadvantage, compared to many other animals.

MAN IS ONE OF THE MOST ADAPTABLE OF ALL MAMMALS WHEN IT COMES TO CLIMATE, HE CAN EXIST FROM THE TROPICS TO THE ARCTIC.

THE ONE COMBINATION THAT HE FINDS MOST DANGEROUS TO LIFE IS EXTREME HEAT AND EXTREME ARIDITY— CONDITIONS FOUND IN DESERTS.

THIS COMBINATION OFFERS WARMBLOODED ANIMALS SUCH AS MAN THE PROBLEM OF LOSING HEAT TO A HOT ENVIRONMENT, WHILE MINIMIZING WATER LOSS.

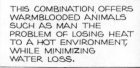

SCIENTISTS HAVE LEARNED MUCH IN THE PAST DECADE ABOUT THE WAY THIS PROBLEM IS HANDLED BY OTHER ANIMALS, WHICH **CAN** SURVIVE IN THE DESERT. . .

WHEN WATER EVAPORATES FROM A SURFACE IT COOLS IT —THUS SWEATING IN WARM-BLOODED ANIMALS KEEPS THE BODY TEMPERATURE WITHIN ACCEPTABLE LIMITS.

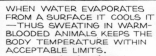

WATER, HOWEVER, IS WHAT DESERT-DWELLING ANIMALS LACK ACCESS TO. THEY CANNOT AFFORD THE LUXURY OF SWEATING TO PREVENT OVERHEATING.

CAMELS GET AROUND THIS BY ALLOWING THEIR BODY TEMPERATURE TO RISE DURING THE DAY FROM 93 DEG. F. TO 105 DEG. F.

THIS STORED HEAT IS LOS BY RADIATION DURING TH COOL NIGHTS, WITHOUT ANY WATER LOSS; HENC THE CAMEL'S LEGENDARY ABILITY TO SURVIVE ARIDITY.

SOME DESERT ANIMALS CONCENTRATE THEIR FAT (AN EFFICIENT INSULATOR), SO THAT MOST OF THE BODY SURFACE CAN ACT AS A RADIATOR TO LOSE HEAT.

t entration

ELEPHANTS HAVE A MOST EFFICIENT RADIATOR IN THE NETWORK OF BLOOD VESSELS BEHIND THEIR EARS—WHICH IS WHY THEY FLAP THEM WHEN HOT.

PANTING IS USED BY MANY DESERT ANIMALS TO LOSE HEAT, BY EVAPORATIVE COOLING FROM A SMALL AREA. THIS CAUSES LESS WATER LOSS THAN BODILY SWEATING.

THE SAHARAN TORTOISE USES THERMOREGULATORY SALIVATION. COPIOUS SALIVA WETS THE HEAD, NECK, AND FRONT LEGS, AND COOLS THEM BY EVAPORATION.

DESERT SNAILS HAVE A LETHAL TEMPERATURE OF 0 DEG. F., BUT EASILY SURVIVE IN SUROUNDINGS FAR ABOVE THIS LEVEL.

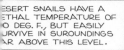

snail

air space

140 deg. F.

ONE REASON IS THAT THIS SNAIL HAS AN AIR SPACE IN ITS SHELL, WHICH ISOLATES AND INSULATES THE ANIMAL FROM CONTACT WITH HOT ROCKS.

IT ALSO CUTS DOWN ITS WATER LOSS SO EFFICIENTLY THAT ONE DRINK DURING THE RAINY SEASON CAN LAST IT FOR SEVERAL YEARS. . .

OSTRICHES, ON THE OTHER HAND, KEEP COOL BY EVAPORATING WATER COPIOUSLY. THEY CAN OBTAIN SUFFICIENT BY DRINKING 20 PER CENT SEAWATER, EXCRETING THE SALT THROUGH A SPECIAL NASAL GLAND.

EXTREME HEAT AND ARIDITY, MAN LOSES WATER FROM THE BLOOD, WHICH THICKENS, UNTIL ABOUT 10 PER CENT OF BODY WEIGHT IS LOST.

THE BLOOD THEN CANNOT CIRCULATE QUICKLY ENOUGH TO CARRY AWAY HEAT FROM THE MUSCLES, AND "EXPLOSIVE HEAT DEATH" FOLLOWS IMMEDIATELY.

THE CAMEL, HOWEVER, HAS A PHYSIOLOGICAL MECHANISM WHICH ENSURES THAT WATER IS FIRST LOST FROM THE TISSUES, WHILE THE BLOOD VOLUME REMAINS CONSTANT.

SUCH DISCOVERIES ARE HELPING SCIENCE DEVISE WAYS TO HELP MEN SURVIVE IN DESERTS, THE MOST INHOSPITABLE OF ALL REGIONS FOR HUMAN LIFE. . .

The heat-proof oryx

One of the most successful adaptions to hot and arid conditio
is shown by an African antelope, which exists in the desert witho
ever drinking water at all.

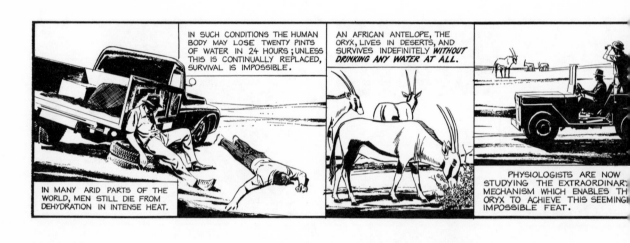

IN MANY ARID PARTS OF THE WORLD, MEN STILL DIE FROM DEHYDRATION IN INTENSE HEAT.

IN SUCH CONDITIONS THE HUMAN BODY MAY LOSE TWENTY PINTS OF WATER IN 24 HOURS; UNLESS THIS IS CONTINUALLY REPLACED, SURVIVAL IS IMPOSSIBLE.

AN AFRICAN ANTELOPE, THE ORYX, LIVES IN DESERTS, AND SURVIVES INDEFINITELY *WITHOUT DRINKING ANY WATER AT ALL.*

PHYSIOLOGISTS ARE NOW STUDYING THE EXTRAORDINAR MECHANISM WHICH ENABLES TH ORYX TO ACHIEVE THIS SEEMING IMPOSSIBLE FEAT.

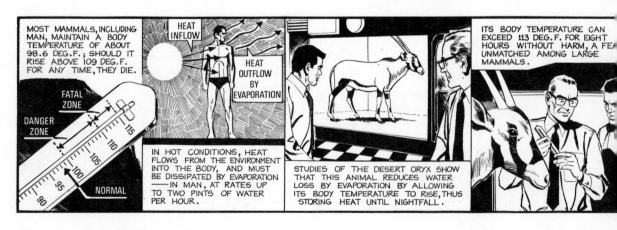

MOST MAMMALS, INCLUDING MAN, MAINTAIN A BODY TEMPERATURE OF ABOUT 98.6 DEG.F.; SHOULD IT RISE ABOVE 109 DEG.F. FOR ANY TIME, THEY DIE.

FATAL ZONE

DANGER ZONE

115
110
105
100
95
90

NORMAL

HEAT INFLOW

HEAT OUTFLOW BY EVAPORATION

IN HOT CONDITIONS, HEAT FLOWS FROM THE ENVIRONMENT INTO THE BODY, AND MUST BE DISSIPATED BY EVAPORATION —— IN MAN, AT RATES UP TO TWO PINTS OF WATER PER HOUR.

STUDIES OF THE DESERT ORYX SHOW THAT THIS ANIMAL REDUCES WATER LOSS BY EVAPORATION BY ALLOWING ITS BODY TEMPERATURE TO RISE, THUS STORING HEAT UNTIL NIGHTFALL.

ITS BODY TEMPERATURE CAN EXCEED 113 DEG.F. FOR EIGHT HOURS WITHOUT HARM, A FE UNMATCHED AMONG LARGE MAMMALS.

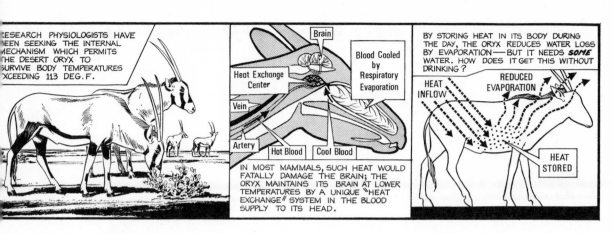

RESEARCH PHYSIOLOGISTS HAVE BEEN SEEKING THE INTERNAL MECHANISM WHICH PERMITS THE DESERT ORYX TO SURVIVE BODY TEMPERATURES EXCEEDING 113 DEG. F.

Brain

Heat Exchange Center

Vein

Artery

Hot Blood

Cool Blood

Blood Cooled by Respiratory Evaporation

IN MOST MAMMALS, SUCH HEAT WOULD FATALLY DAMAGE THE BRAIN; THE ORYX MAINTAINS ITS BRAIN AT LOWER TEMPERATURES BY A UNIQUE "HEAT EXCHANGE" SYSTEM IN THE BLOOD SUPPLY TO ITS HEAD.

BY STORING HEAT IN ITS BODY DURING THE DAY, THE ORYX REDUCES WATER LOSS BY EVAPORATION—BUT IT NEEDS *SOME* WATER. HOW DOES IT GET THIS WITHOUT DRINKING?

HEAT INFLOW

REDUCED EVAPORATION

HEAT STORED

THE DESERT ORYX REQUIRES ABOUT 4 PINTS OF WATER PER DAY TO STAY ALIVE, EVEN WITH ITS MECHANISMS FOR REDUCING WATER LOSS BY EVAPORATION.

AS THERE IS NO WATER IN ITS DESERT HABITAT, IT MUST GET THIS DAILY WATER INTAKE FROM WHAT IT EATS.

ANALYSIS OF ITS FAVORITE SHRUB, HOWEVER, SHOWS IT TO CONTAIN LESS THAN 1 PER CENT WATER; THE LEAVES ARE SO DRY THEY FALL APART AT A TOUCH.

IT WOULD BE IMPOSSIBLE FOR AN ORYX TO EAT ENOUGH OF SUCH FOOD TO OBTAIN ITS WATER REQUIREMENTS; HOW CAN THIS CONTRADICTION BE EXPLAINED?

PHYSIOLOGISTS NOW BELIEVE THAT THE DESERT ORYX SURVIVES IN THE DESERT WITHOUT DRINKING BY FEEDING ONLY AT NIGHT.

THE PLANTS IT EATS—ALMOST TOTALLY DRY BY DAY—CAN ABSORB UP TO 30 PER CENT WATER AT NIGHT, WHEN THE TEMPERATURE DROP CAUSES A RISE IN RELATIVE AIR HUMIDITY.

DAY
1% Water

NIGHT
30% Water

WITH ITS MECHANISM FOR REDUCING EVAPORATIVE WATER LOSS, THE ORYX CAN THEREFORE SURVIVE IN DESERT CONDITIONS FATAL FOR OTHER MAMMALS.

THE FARMING OF THIS ANIMAL, IN AREAS UNSUITABLE FOR OTHER BEASTS, MIGHT ONE DAY HELP TO INCREASE AFRICA'S PROTEIN SUPPLIES...

Fish with warm blood

Contrary to general belief, some specialized ocean-dwelling fish maintain their body temperature many degrees above the water temperature.

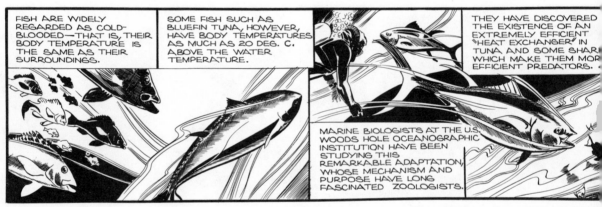

FISH ARE WIDELY REGARDED AS COLD-BLOODED—THAT IS, THEIR BODY TEMPERATURE IS THE SAME AS THEIR SURROUNDINGS.

SOME FISH SUCH AS BLUEFIN TUNA, HOWEVER, HAVE BODY TEMPERATURES AS MUCH AS 20 DEG. C. ABOVE THE WATER TEMPERATURE.

THEY HAVE DISCOVERED THE EXISTENCE OF AN EXTREMELY EFFICIENT "HEAT EXCHANGER" IN TUNA AND SOME SHARKS WHICH MAKE THEM MORE EFFICIENT PREDATORS.

MARINE BIOLOGISTS AT THE U.S. WOODS HOLE OCEANOGRAPHIC INSTITUTION HAVE BEEN STUDYING THIS REMARKABLE ADAPTATION, WHOSE MECHANISM AND PURPOSE HAVE LONG FASCINATED ZOOLOGISTS.

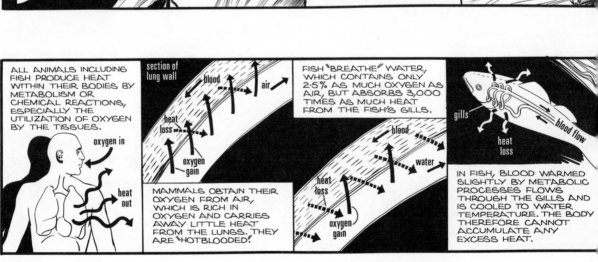

ALL ANIMALS INCLUDING FISH PRODUCE HEAT WITHIN THEIR BODIES BY METABOLISM OR CHEMICAL REACTIONS, ESPECIALLY THE UTILIZATION OF OXYGEN BY THE TISSUES.

oxygen in

heat out

section of lung wall

blood

air

heat loss

oxygen gain

MAMMALS OBTAIN THEIR OXYGEN FROM AIR, WHICH IS RICH IN OXYGEN AND CARRIES AWAY LITTLE HEAT FROM THE LUNGS. THEY ARE "HOTBLOODED."

FISH "BREATHE" WATER, WHICH CONTAINS ONLY 2·5% AS MUCH OXYGEN AS AIR, BUT ABSORBS 3,000 TIMES AS MUCH HEAT FROM THE FISH'S GILLS.

blood

heat loss

water

oxygen gain

gills

heat loss

blood flow

IN FISH, BLOOD WARMED SLIGHTLY BY METABOLIC PROCESSES FLOWS THROUGH THE GILLS AND IS COOLED TO WATER TEMPERATURE. THE BODY THEREFORE CANNOT ACCUMULATE ANY EXCESS HEAT.

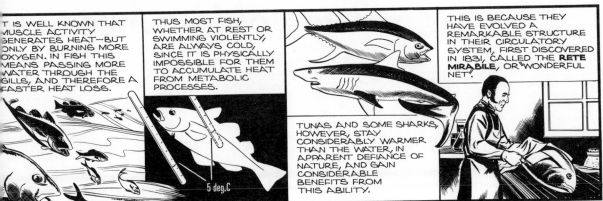

IT IS WELL KNOWN THAT MUSCLE ACTIVITY GENERATES HEAT—BUT ONLY BY BURNING MORE OXYGEN. IN FISH THIS MEANS PASSING MORE WATER THROUGH THE GILLS, AND THEREFORE A FASTER HEAT LOSS.

THUS MOST FISH, WHETHER AT REST OR SWIMMING VIOLENTLY, ARE ALWAYS COLD, SINCE IT IS PHYSICALLY IMPOSSIBLE FOR THEM TO ACCUMULATE HEAT FROM METABOLIC PROCESSES.

5 deg.C

TUNAS AND SOME SHARKS, HOWEVER, STAY CONSIDERABLY WARMER THAN THE WATER, IN APPARENT DEFIANCE OF NATURE, AND GAIN CONSIDERABLE BENEFITS FROM THIS ABILITY.

THIS IS BECAUSE THEY HAVE EVOLVED A REMARKABLE STRUCTURE IN THEIR CIRCULATORY SYSTEM, FIRST DISCOVERED IN 1831, CALLED THE **RETE MIRABILE**, OR "WONDERFUL NET."

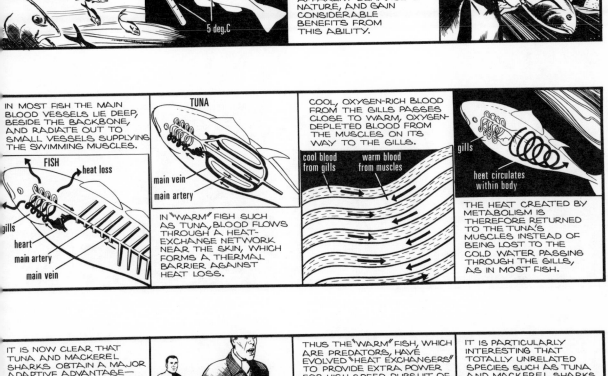

IN MOST FISH THE MAIN BLOOD VESSELS LIE DEEP, BESIDE THE BACKBONE, AND RADIATE OUT TO SMALL VESSELS SUPPLYING THE SWIMMING MUSCLES.

FISH
heat loss
gills
heart
main artery
main vein

TUNA
main vein
main artery

IN "WARM" FISH SUCH AS TUNA, BLOOD FLOWS THROUGH A HEAT-EXCHANGE NETWORK NEAR THE SKIN, WHICH FORMS A THERMAL BARRIER AGAINST HEAT LOSS.

COOL, OXYGEN-RICH BLOOD FROM THE GILLS PASSES CLOSE TO WARM, OXYGEN-DEPLETED BLOOD FROM THE MUSCLES ON ITS WAY TO THE GILLS.

cool blood from gills   warm blood from muscles

gills
heat circulates within body

THE HEAT CREATED BY METABOLISM IS THEREFORE RETURNED TO THE TUNA'S MUSCLES INSTEAD OF BEING LOST TO THE COLD WATER PASSING THROUGH THE GILLS, AS IN MOST FISH.

IT IS NOW CLEAR THAT TUNA AND MACKEREL SHARKS OBTAIN A MAJOR ADAPTIVE ADVANTAGE—ENHANCED MUSCLE POWER—FROM THEIR RAISED BODY TEMPERATURE.

AS BETWEEN TWO SIMILAR MUSCLES, ONE WHICH IS 10 DEG.C. WARMER THAN THE OTHER CAN FLEX THREE TIMES MORE RAPIDLY AND GENERATE THREE TIMES MORE POWER —A FACT WELL KNOWN TO ATHLETES.

THUS THE "WARM" FISH, WHICH ARE PREDATORS, HAVE EVOLVED "HEAT EXCHANGERS" TO PROVIDE EXTRA POWER FOR HIGH-SPEED PURSUIT OF FAST-MOVING PREY: A BLUEFIN TUNA CAN BRIEFLY EXCEED 40 MPH.

IT IS PARTICULARLY INTERESTING THAT TOTALLY UNRELATED SPECIES SUCH AS TUNA AND MACKEREL SHARKS HAVE INDEPENDENTLY EVOLVED THE SAME MECHANISM. . .

The coldest mamma

Scientists are increasingly interested in the activities of Weddell seal, which exhibits unusual adaptions to life beneath Antarctic ice.

IN 1825 THE ANTARCTIC EXPLORER JAMES WEDDELL DISCOVERED A WARM-BLOODED MAMMAL THAT LIVES AND THRIVES IN UNBELIEVABLY ARDUOUS CONDITIONS —— THE WEDDELL SEAL, NOW NAMED AFTER HIM.

THIS ANIMAL SURVIVES AIR TEMPERATURES OF -70 F., WATER TEMPERATURES AROUND 28 F., AND MUST FIND ITS FOOD UNDER THE ICE.

MORE REMARKABLY, IT CAN SWIM FOR MORE THAN AN HOUR WITHOUT COMING UP FOR AIR, AND FINDS ITS BREATHING HOLES EVEN IN TOTAL DARKNESS.

THESE FACTORS, TOGETHER WITH ITS ABILITY TO "CRASH DIVE" TO 1800 FT. WITHOUT HARM, HAVE MADE THE WEDDELL SEAL A PRIME STUDY FOR ZOOLOGISTS.

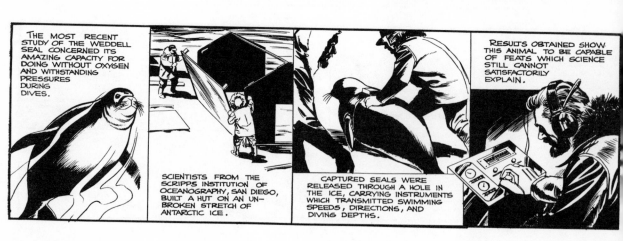

THE MOST RECENT STUDY OF THE WEDDELL SEAL CONCERNED ITS AMAZING CAPACITY FOR DOING WITHOUT OXYGEN AND WITHSTANDING PRESSURES DURING DIVES.

SCIENTISTS FROM THE SCRIPPS INSTITUTION OF OCEANOGRAPHY, SAN DIEGO, BUILT A HUT ON AN UN-BROKEN STRETCH OF ANTARCTIC ICE.

CAPTURED SEALS WERE RELEASED THROUGH A HOLE IN THE ICE, CARRYING INSTRUMENTS WHICH TRANSMITTED SWIMMING SPEEDS, DIRECTIONS, AND DIVING DEPTHS.

RESULTS OBTAINED SHOW THIS ANIMAL TO BE CAPABLE OF FEATS WHICH SCIENCE STILL CANNOT SATISFACTORILY EXPLAIN.

SCIENTISTS IN THE ANTARCTIC HAVE FOUND THE WEDDELL SEAL CAPABLE OF DIVING STRAIGHT DOWN TO 1,800 FT. AND UP AGAIN WITHIN 12 MINUTES.

DURING SUCH DIVES IT DESCENDS AND ASCENDS AT 360 FT. PER MINUTE WITHOUT ILL EFFECT TO ITS LUNGS OR EARS.

OTHER MAMMALS, SUCH AS MAN, WOULD SUFFER CRUSHING OF THE LUNGS AND WINDPIPE IF, LIKE THE SEAL, THEY CONTAINED AIR AT ATMOSPHERIC PRESSURE.

THE SEAL'S WINDPIPE, HOWEVER, CAN BE FLATTENED BY PRESSURE WITHOUT DAMAGE — A UNIQUE NATURAL ADAPTATION TO ITS NEEDS.

SEAL

Normal

Under pressure

HUMAN

ONE STILL UNEXPLAINED MYSTERY IS HOW THE WEDDELL SEAL CAN RISE RAPIDLY FROM 1,800 FT. WITHOUT GETTING "THE BENDS" WHICH AFFECTS DIVERS WHO SURFACE TOO SUDDENLY.

BENDS ARE CAUSED BY NITROGEN, DISSOLVED IN THE BLOOD BY THE PRESSURE, TURNING INTO BUBBLES AS THE PRESSURE IS REMOVED.

LUNGS UNDER PRESSURE

APPARENTLY THE SEAL'S LUNGS COLLAPSE COMPLETELY AT DEPTH, DRIVING THE GASES INTO THE BRONCHIAL PASSAGES, WHERE THE NITROGEN CANNOT BE ABSORBED INTO THE BLOOD.

AS THIS ALSO DEPRIVES IT OF OXYGEN, THE SEAL REDUCES ITS HEARTBEAT TO ONE TENTH NORMAL WHEN DIVING, AND SHUTS DOWN BLOOD SUPPLIES TO ALL TISSUES EXCEPT THE HEART, FLIPPERS, AND BRAIN.

EVEN MORE REMARKABLE THAN THE WEDDELL SEAL'S DIVING CAPACITY IS ITS UNDER-WATER NAVIGATION ABILITY, EVEN IN TOTAL DARKNESS.

IT CAN SWIM FOR ONE HOUR UNDER THE ICE; IF IT DOES NOT FIND ANOTHER BREATHING HOLE IT UNERRINGLY RETURNS TO WHERE IT STARTED FROM.

ZOOLOGISTS ARE PUZZLED HOW THE SEAL KNOWS WHEN IT HAS REACHED THE "POINT OF NO RETURN", AND MUST TURN BACK.

SUCH FASCINATING QUESTIONS ARE INCREASINGLY ATTRACTING SCIENTISTS TO THE UNIQUE BIOLOGICAL LABORATORY OF THE ANTARCTIC.

Freedom from friction

Many animals, particularly some that live in the sea, can mo through their liquid medium with a freedom from friction that mode technology cannot equal.

THE DEPARTMENT OF ANIMAL STUDY AT KIEL UNIVERSITY NOW RECEIVES THE BODY OF ANY DOLPHIN WHICH DIES IN GERMAN AQUARIUMS.

BIOLOGISTS THERE ARE COOPERATING WITH SHIP-BUILDING RESEARCH INSTITUTES IN BERLIN AND HAMBURG TO IMPROVE THE DESIGN OF SHIPS.

CREATURES WHICH MOVE FAST IN WATER OR AIR — BIRDS, FISH, SEALS, DOLPHINS — HAVE SPECIAL SURFACE CHARACTERISTICS FOR BEATING FRICTION.

SCIENTISTS IN MANY COUNTR ARE NOW STUDYING THES BIOLOGICAL MODELS FOR WAYS OF REDUCING DRAG IN SHIPS AND AIRCRAFT.

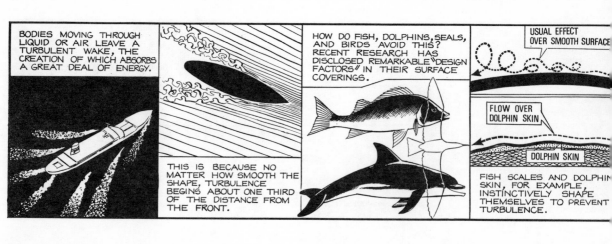

BODIES MOVING THROUGH LIQUID OR AIR LEAVE A TURBULENT WAKE, THE CREATION OF WHICH ABSORBS A GREAT DEAL OF ENERGY.

THIS IS BECAUSE NO MATTER HOW SMOOTH THE SHAPE, TURBULENCE BEGINS ABOUT ONE THIRD OF THE DISTANCE FROM THE FRONT.

HOW DO FISH, DOLPHINS, SEALS, AND BIRDS AVOID THIS? RECENT RESEARCH HAS DISCLOSED REMARKABLE "DESIGN FACTORS" IN THEIR SURFACE COVERINGS.

USUAL EFFECT OVER SMOOTH SURFACE

FLOW OVER DOLPHIN SKIN

DOLPHIN SKIN

FISH SCALES AND DOLPHIN SKIN, FOR EXAMPLE, INSTINCTIVELY SHAPE THEMSELVES TO PREVENT TURBULENCE.

SCIENTISTS HAVE DISCOVERED THAT UNDER THE DOLPHIN'S HARD SKIN LIES A CUSHION OF OIL, WHICH YIELDS TO THE SLIGHTEST PRESSURE.

SKIN
OIL
TISSUE
PRESSURE

FLOW ON SMOOTH SURFACE
ACTUAL FLOW

THE SKIN THUS SHAPES ITSELF TO TURBULENCE IN ITS FORMATIVE STAGE, PREVENTING IT FROM BUILDING UP AND CAUSING DRAG.

FISH SCALES ARE ALSO FLEXIBLE, AND HAVE THE SAME EFFECT; BUT FISH HAVE AN EVEN MORE INGENIOUS SLIMY COATING.

MADE UP OF VISCOUS POLYURON ACIDS, THIS ACTUALLY REDUCES FRICTION BY TRAILING TINY THREADS THROUGH THE WATER...

VISCOUS THREADS
(Enlarged)

WATER FLOW

FISH CONTINUALLY EXUDE VISCOUS ACIDS, WHICH ARE DRAWN OUT INTO THREADS BY THE PASSAGE OF THE FISH THROUGH THE WATER.

THESE ACT LIKE THIN PARALLEL TUBES, ALLOWING WATER TO FLOW STRAIGHT BACK, BUT DISCOURAGING MOVEMENT IN OTHER DIRECTIONS — THUS PREVENTING TURBULENCE.

WATER FLOW
THREADS

SCIENTISTS ARE GETTING THE SAME EFFECT WITH "LONG-CHAIN POLYMERS"—STRINGS OF LINKED SYNTHETIC MOLECULES.

BY SLOWLY RELEASING SUCH SUBSTANCES THROUGH POROUS SURFACES, THEY HAVE REDUCED FRICTION DRAG BY AS MUCH AS 7.0 PER CENT.

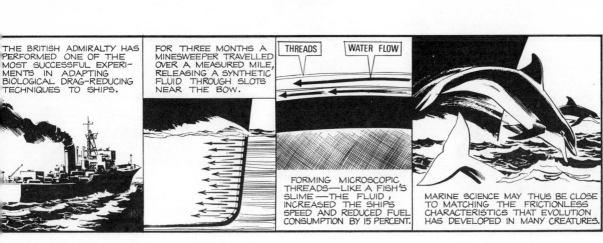

THE BRITISH ADMIRALTY HAS PERFORMED ONE OF THE MOST SUCCESSFUL EXPERIMENTS IN ADAPTING BIOLOGICAL DRAG-REDUCING TECHNIQUES TO SHIPS.

FOR THREE MONTHS A MINESWEEPER TRAVELLED OVER A MEASURED MILE, RELEASING A SYNTHETIC FLUID THROUGH SLOTS NEAR THE BOW.

THREADS
WATER FLOW

FORMING MICROSCOPIC THREADS—LIKE A FISH'S SLIME—THE FLUID, INCREASED THE SHIPS SPEED AND REDUCED FUEL CONSUMPTION BY 15 PERCENT.

MARINE SCIENCE MAY THUS BE CLOSE TO MATCHING THE FRICTIONLESS CHARACTERISTICS THAT EVOLUTION HAS DEVELOPED IN MANY CREATURES.

The survival techniques of bees

Bees have solved the problems of living in large, crowded communities with a success that some human societies might envy.

THE EXTRAORDINARY SOCIAL ORGANIZATION AND COLLECTIVE INTELLIGENCE OF BEES HAS INTRIGUED SCIENTISTS FOR CENTURIES.

FOR EXAMPLE, EXPERIMENTS HAVE NOW PROVED THAT FORAGING BEES SIGNAL TO OTHER BEES IN THE HIVE THE DIRECTION AND DISTANCE OF NECTAR SOURCES BY A FIGURE-8 DANCE.

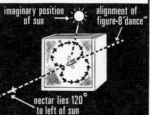

imaginary position of sun   alignment of figure-8 "dance"

nectar lies 120° to left of sun

RECENT STUDIES HAVE YIELDED NEW EVIDENCE OF THE REMARKABLE WAY IN WHICH BEES MAINTAIN THE ENVIRONMENT INSIDE THE HIVE, WHEN FACED WITH PROBLEMS VERY SIMILAR TO OURS.

THEY EFFICIENTLY REGULATE TEMPERATURE AND HUMIDITY, ELIMINATE POLLUTED AIR, REMOVE FOREIGN OBJECTS AND DEAD BODIES, AND CONTROL BACTERIA THAT ATTACK THEM AND THEIR FOOD. . .

AN AVERAGE COLONY OF BEES—PERHAPS 50,000 INDIVIDUALS—IS CROWDED TOGETHER MUCH MORE THAN ANY HUMAN POPULATION, AND YET SURVIVES MANY POTENTIALLY DESTRUCTIVE FACTORS.

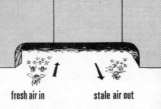

fresh air in   stale air out

BEES VENTILATE THE HIVE, FOR EXAMPLE, BY FANNING FRESH AIR IN. THIS KEEPS THE TEMPERATURE AROUND 92 DEG. F. FOR ABOUT 10 MONTHS, WHILE BROOD ARE BEING REARED.

THIS COOLING ALSO PLAYS AN IMPORTANT PART IN MAKING HONEY, WHICH FOR PROPER STORAGE MUST HAVE A WATER CONTENT OF NO MORE THAN 19%.

NECTAR GATHERED FROM FLOWERS MAY BE UP TO 90% WATER; THE EXCESS IS EVAPORATED BY BLOWING AIR OVER THE NECTAR IN THE COMB CELLS.

bees fanning wings

SINCE BEES EAT ONLY HONEY AND POLLEN (RICH IN PROTEIN AND FATS), THE PROTECTION OF THESE STORED FOODS AGAINST BACTERIAL SPOILAGE IS CRUCIAL.

THIS REMARKABLE BACTERICIDAL ACTION WAS NOT FINALLY EXPLAINED UNTIL 1962, WHEN HONEY WAS FOUND TO CONTAIN THE ENZYME GLUCOSE OXIDASE, ADDED BY WORKER BEES.

THIS ENZYME REACTS WITH GLUCOSE IN THE HONEY, RELEASING HYDROGEN PEROXIDE—A POWERFUL GERM-KILLER...

EARLY THIS CENTURY RESEARCHERS FOUND THAT 10 HARMFUL MICROORGANISMS (INCLUDING THOSE CAUSING TYPHOID AND DYSENTERY), WHEN ADDED TO HONEY, WERE KILLED WITHIN 48 HOURS.

BEES HAVE INGENIOUS MECHANISMS FOR PROTECTING STORED POLLEN: THEY FILL POLLEN CELLS TO ONLY 80% OF THEIR DEPTH (ALTHOUGH HONEY CELLS ARE FILLED TO THE BRIM).

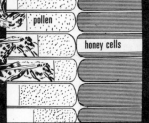

pollen

honey cells

DURING THE SPRING BROOD-REARING ACTIVITY, THE POLLEN STORES ARE TURNED OVER RAPIDLY, AND SO THE RISK OF BACTERIAL SPOILAGE IS LOW.

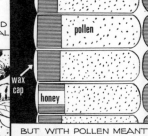

pollen

wax cap

honey

BUT WITH POLLEN MEANT TO BE KEPT THROUGH THE WINTER, THE SPACE IN THE CELL IS FILLED WITH HONEY AND SEALED WITH WAX.

BEES ALSO STORE POLLEN BY COLOR. EACH CELL CONTAINS A GIVEN COLOR, BUT IN A SCATTERED PATTERN. FOOD FROM DIFFERENT SOURCES IS THUS KEPT SEPARATE, IN CASE ONE SOURCE HAS POOR STORAGE QUALITIES.

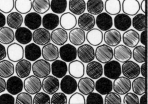

DURING SUMMER A WORKER BEE'S LIFESPAN IS ABOUT 5 WEEKS, AND IN A COLONY THEY DIE AT THE RATE OF PERHAPS 1,000 BEES PER DAY—BUT DEAD BEES ARE RARE NEAR THE HIVE.

THUS WHEN THEY DIE THEY ARE USUALLY FAR FROM THE HIVE, WHICH IS THUS SPARED THE SANITATION PROBLEM OF DISPOSAL OF THOUSANDS OF DEAD BEES.

THIS IS BECAUSE WORKERS START THEIR LIVES WITH HIVE DUTIES, SUCH AS COMB BUILDING, AND IN OLD AGE GRADUATE TO THE HEAVIEST WORK: NECTAR FORAGING.

SUCH ARE SOME OF THE WAYS THAT BEE COLONIES HANDLE MANY OF THE PROBLEMS FACED, WITH MOUNTING CONCERN, BY CROWDED HUMAN POPULATIONS...

Chemical warfare by insect.

Among the unusual defence mechanism evolved in the natur
world is the explosive apparatus of the bombarding beetle.

IN MANY COUNTRIES TODAY, CHEMICAL WARFARE IS THE SUBJECT OF EXTENSIVE SCIENTIFIC RESEARCH.

ALTHOUGH PUBLIC OPINION IS DIVIDED, THE MAJOR POWERS ARE DEVELOPING CHEMICAL WEAPONS, ESPECIALLY GASES.

CHEMICAL WARFARE ITSELF, HOWEVER, IS NOT NEW —— IT IS FOUND IN MANY INSECTS, AN EVOLUTIONARY DEFENCE MECHANISM TO REPEL ENEMIES.

AS LONG AGO AS 1752 THE GERMAN ENTOMOLOGIST DE BEER DESCRIBED THE UNIQUE CAPACITY OF THE "BOMBARDING BEETLE," WHICH HAS A REMARK- ABLY SOPHISTICATED GAS - FIRING MECHANISM...

RECENT RESEARCH AT HEIDELBERG UNIVERSITY, W. GERMANY, SHOWS THAT THE CHEMICAL WARFARE EQUIPMENT OF THE HUMBLE "BOMB- ARDING BEETLE" (BRACHYNIDEN) IS AS COMPLEX, IN ITS OWN WAY, AS MANY MAN- MADE WEAPONS.

IT CONSISTS OF A "FIRING CHAMBER," AS IN A ROCKET, WHICH CAN BE SUPPLIED WITH A MIXTURE OF "FUELS" FROM SEPARATE GLANDS.

ITS CHIEF FUEL IS A 28 PER CENT SOLUTION OF HYDROGEN PEROXIDE —— A POWERFUL COMPOUND WIDELY USED IN INDUSTRY AS A BLEACH.

THIS SOLUTION CONTAINS HYDROCHINONE, ITSELF HARMLESS BUT RELATED TO THE HIGHLY IRRITANT CHINONE (CARRIED B SOME OTHER BEETLES) WHICH BURNS THE SKIN.

HYDROGEN PEROXIDE, THE MAIN FUEL OF THE BOMBARDING BEETLE, IS A PRODUCT OF META-BOLISM, AND HIGHLY POISONOUS.

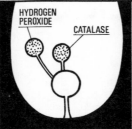

HYDROGEN PEROXIDE   CATALASE

LIVING THINGS NEUTRALIZE IT BY CIRCULATING THE ENZYME CATALASE; THIS BEETLE, HOWEVER, STORES UP BOTH HYDROGEN PEROXIDE AND CATALASE IN SEPARATE TANKS.

IN ANOTHER SET OF GLANDS IT KEEPS THE ENZYME PEROXIDASE; ALL TANKS ARE CONNECTED TO A FIRING CHAMBER.

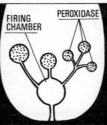

FIRING CHAMBER   PEROXIDASE

WHEN THREATENED BY AN ENEMY, THE BEETLE QUICKLY PUMPS ALL THESE LIQUIDS INTO THE COMBUSTION CHAMBER —— AND VIOLENT REACTIONS OCCUR...

WHEN THE BOMBARDING BEETLE PUMPS ITS VARIOUS FUELS INTO ITS COMBUST-ON CHAMBER, POWERFUL CHEMICAL REACTIONS TAKE PLACE INSTANTLY.

HYDROGEN PEROXIDE + HYDROCHINONE   PEROXIDASE

CATALASE

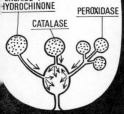

CATALASE DECOMPOSES HYDROGEN PEROXIDE INTO WATER AND OXYGEN GAS; PEROXIDASE TRANSFORMS HARMLESS HYDROCHINONE INTO AGGRESSIVE CHINONE.

GAS PRESSURE BUILDING UP

THE RESULTING PRESSURE AND HEAT BUILD UP INTO AN EXPLOSION, WHICH FIRES THE IRRITANT MIXTURE OUT OF THE BEETLE TOWARDS ITS PURSUER.

THE BEETLE'S TANKS CARRY ENOUGH LIQUIDS TO FIRE TWELVE "SHOTS" IN SUCCESSION; IT THEN REQUIRES AN HOUR TO SECRETE MORE...

AS WELL AS THOSE CARRYING POWERFUL REPELLANTS TO PROTECT THEMSELVES, THERE ARE SOME BEETLES WITH CHEMICALS WHICH ASSIST THEM TO ESCAPE.

ONE SMALL LAND BEETLE, WHICH SOMETIMES GOES ON WATER, CAN MAKE A RAPID "ASSISTED PASSAGE" BACK TO SAFETY IF THREATENED BY A BIRD.

IT EMITS A GROUP OF OILY COMPOUNDS WHICH INSTANTLY SPREAD OUT, FORMING A THIN FILM WHICH PUSHES ASIDE ANYTHING IN THE WAY —— INCLUDING THE BEETLE!

THIS HAPPENS SO SUDDENLY THAT THE BEETLE IS PROPELLED TO THE SAFETY OF THE SHORE BY CHEMICAL MOTIVE POWER...

The quick change locus

The plague locust lives a strange double life, at times solit
and harmless, at other times gregarious and a menace to wh
continents.

WHEN, SOME 9,000 YEARS AGO, PRIMITIVE MAN BEGAN TO CULTIVATE WILD PLANTS FOR FOOD, HE MUST HAVE ENCOUNTERED A VORACIOUS INSECT PEST — THE LOCUST

THE EARLIEST RECORD OF THIS ENEMY OF AGRICULTURE IS FOUND IN EGYPTIAN CARVINGS, DATED ABOUT 2,400 B.C.

ENTOMOLOGISTS ARE STILL NOT COMPLETELY CERTAIN WHY LOCUST PLAGUES ERUPT THE WAY THEY DO . . .

. . . BUT TODAY THEY ARE LEARNING MORE ABOUT THE REMARKABLE BE-HAVIOR PATTERNS OF THE WORLD'S NUMBER ONE THREAT TO FOOD PRODUCT

MORE MONEY HAS BEEN SPENT ON LOCUST CONTROL AND RESEARCH THAN ON ANY OTHER SINGLE INSECT IN THE HISTORY OF MAN.

LOCUSTS ARE SIMILAR TO CRICKETS AND GRASS-HOPPERS, BUT HAVE TWO IMPORTANT (AND DANGER-OUS) CHARACTERISTICS: SWARMING AND MOVEMENT.

LOCUSTS REACT TO EACH OTHER BY FORMING EVER LARGER GROUPS: A TYPICAL SWARM MAY CONTAIN 70 MILLION INSECTS PER SQUARE KILOMETER.

SWARMS OF 1000 SQ. KILOMETERS HAVE BEEN MEASURED — WHICH MEAN PERHAPS 40,000 MILLION INSECTS, EACH EATING ITS OWN WEIGHT OF FOOD PER DAY . . . .

A LARGE SWARM OF LOCUSTS CAN EAT 80,000 TONS OF FOOD EVERY DAY — ENOUGH GRAIN TO FEED 400,000 PEOPLE FOR ONE YEAR.

SINCE A SWARM CAN MOVE UP TO 50 MILES A DAY, AND MAY TRAVEL THOUSANDS OF MILES BEFORE DYING OUT AS MYSTERIOUSLY AS IT FORMED, THE DESTRUCTION IS ENORMOUS

THE MECHANISM OF SWARM FORMATION AND THE MIGRATORY DRIVE REMAINED A MYSTERY TO SCIENCE UNTIL EARLY IN THIS CENTURY...

...WHEN TWO ENTOMOLOGISTS INDEPENDENTLY DISCOVERED A REMARKABLE FACT ABOUT THE LOCUST: IT EXISTS IN TWO FORMS, DIFFERENT IN SIZE, SHAPE, COLOR, AND BEHAVIOR.

ABOUT 1921 TWO SCIENTISTS — UVAROV, RUSSIAN, AND FAURE, SOUTH AFRICAN — INDEPENDENTLY REACHED A FASCINATING CONCLUSION ABOUT LOCUSTS.

IT HAD BEEN NOTICED THAT AFTER A SWARM OF MIGRATORY LOCUSTS LEFT AN AREA THERE WAS OFTEN FOUND ANOTHER, GRASSHOPPER—LIKE INSECT THAT WAS SOLITARY AND NON—MIGRATORY.

UVAROV AND FAURE DISCOVERED THAT THIS INSECT, ALTHOUGH QUITE DIFFERENT IN APPEARANCE, WAS IN FACT THE SAME SPECIES OF LOCUST, LEADING A "DOUBLE LIFE"!

FURTHERMORE, IT COULD BE CONVERTED IN THE LABORATORY FROM THE HARMLESS TO THE RAVENOUS FORM, AND BACK AGAIN, IN A MATTER OF DAYS...

THE DISCOVERY IN 1921 OF THE LOCUST'S TWO PHASES — ITS "JEKYLL AND HYDE" EXISTENCE — OPENED A NEW ERA IN THE UNDERSTANDING OF THIS MENACE TO THE WORLD'S AGRICULTURE.

FOR THE FIRST TIME SCIENTISTS SAW A CHANCE TO FIND OUT WHY LOCUSTS INEXPLICABLY FORM ENORMOUS SWARMS AND BEGIN TO MOVE...

THE MECHANISM IS NOW CLEAR: THE SWARM BEGINS WITH COMPARATIVELY FEW SOLITARY, SEDENTARY INSECTS, WHICH SUDDENLY CHANGE IN SIZE, SHAPE, COLOR, AND BEHAVIOR.

NOW THE SEARCH IS ON FOR THE ANSWER TO THE LOCUST PLAGUES THAT EXPLODE ACROSS EVERY CONTINENT EXCEPT THE ICE-CAPS AND NORTH AMERICA.

Checking the plague locus

A world-wide scientific campaign is steadily improving techniques for preventing the plague locust from developing its w known swarming behavior.

THE BREAKTHROUGH IN CONTROL OF MANKIND'S NO. 1 AGRICULTURAL PEST — THE LOCUST — WAS THE DISCOVERY OF THE INSECT'S DUAL EXISTENCE.

IN ITS QUIET PHASE, THE LOCUST SHUNS ITS OWN SPECIES AND HARDLY MOVES ABOUT.

HOWEVER, IF SEVERAL SUCH INSECTS ARE FORCED INTO EACH OTHER'S COMPANY, THEIR BEHAVIOR CHANGES DRAMATICALLY.

WITHIN 48 HOURS THEY BECOME GREGARIOUS AND SHOW AN OMINOUS URGE T MOVE AND MIGRATE — CHARACTERISTICS OF THE HUNGRY LOCUST PLAGUES

THE DISCOVERY IN 1921 OF LOCUST PHASES SUGGESTED A POSSIBLE EXPLANATION FOR THE SUDDEN APPEARANCE OF LOCUST SWARMS.

DO AREAS EXIST WHERE "SOLITARY" LOCUSTS COLLECT, GRADUALLY CROWD-ING TOGETHER UNTIL THIS CAUSES A "PHASE CHANGE" INTO THE SWARMING VARIETY?

AFRICAN MIGRATORY LOCUST PLAGUES 1928-1941

SYSTEMATIC OBSERVATION AND RECORDING IN MANY COUNTRIES EVENTUALLY DISCLOSED THAT PLAGUES OF SOME SPECIES BEGAN IN SMALL, WELL-DEFINED AREAS.

WORLD ENTOMOLOGISTS THEN BEGAN TO CONCENTRATE THEIR ATTENTION ON THESE OUTBRE/ AREAS — THE KEY TO EFFECTIVE LOCUST CONTROL.

SOMETIMES THEY BREED SUCCESSFULLY AND BECOME CROWDED; THIS LEADS TO "PHASE CHANGE" INTO THE GREGARIOUS, ACTIVE VARIETY.

...OCUST OUTBREAK AREAS ...RE SOMEHOW FAVORABLE ...O THE "SOLITARY PHASE" ...NSECTS, WHICH CAN ALWAYS ...E FOUND THERE.

MULTIPLYING RAPIDLY INTO A VAST SWARM, THE LOCUSTS THEN FLY OUT OF THE OUTBREAK AREA INTO THE INVASION AREA, SEEKING FOOD.

THUS LOCUST SWARMS MIGHT TRAVEL FOR THOUSANDS OF MILES UNTIL THEY DIE FROM LACK OF FOOD — BUT THE "SOLITARY" PHASE ALWAYS REMAINS IN THE OUTBREAK AREAS, READY TO BEGIN THE CYCLE ALL OVER AGAIN.

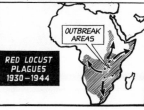

RED LOCUST PLAGUES 1930-1944

OUTBREAK AREAS

THE DISCOVERY OF CERTAIN WELL-DEFINED LOCUST OUTBREAK AREAS ENABLES A CLOSE WATCH TO BE KEPT ON THE "SOLITARY PHASE" INSECTS WHICH LIVE THERE.

AT THE FIRST SIGN OF INCREASING NUMBERS, MODERN TECHNIQUES ARE USED TO CONTROL THEM, THUS PREVENTING CROWDING AND "PHASE CHANGE" INTO SWARMS.

TODAY NO PLAGUES OF AFRICAN MIGRATORY LOCUSTS OR RED LOCUSTS EVER ESCAPE FROM THEIR OUTBREAK AREAS.

BUT THE DESERT LOCUST SPECIES REMAINS A MAJOR PROBLEM, BECASE IT LIVES AND BREEDS OVER A WIDE AREA...

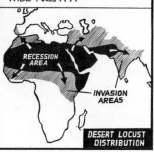

RECESSION AREA

INVASION AREAS

DESERT LOCUST DISTRIBUTION

...ODAY THE LONDON-...ASED DESERT LOCUST ...NFORMATION SERVICE, ...EPRESENTING 40 COUNTRIES, ...ATCHES ALL LOCUST ...OVEMENTS.

RECORDS SHOW THE HUGE FLUCTUATIONS IN LOCUST POPULATIONS, AND THE NUMBER OF COUNTRIES INVADED BY SWARMS.

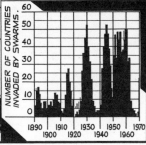

NUMBER OF COUNTRIES INVADED BY SWARMS.
60
50
40
30
20
10
0
1890 1900 1910 1920 1930 1940 1950 1960 1970

IN 1968 AN UPSURGE BEGAN, THREATENING ANOTHER MAJOR OUTBREAK — BUT THE LOCUST INTELLIGENCE CENTER GAVE FOUR MONTHS WARNING.

A GREAT INTERNATIONAL EFFORT INVOLVING MEN, AIRCRAFT, VEHICLES, SPRAY GEAR, AND CHEMICALS KILLED 85 PER CENT OF ALL SWARMS AND AVERTED A PLAGUE — A MAJOR VICTORY IN AN ENDLESS WAR...

Flight control in locusts

Aeronautical scientists are studying the highly sophisticate[d] flight control system of the desert locust, which cannot tell "u[p]" from "down", and yet makes prodigious journeys.

IN THIS AGE OF FLIGHT, SCIENTISTS AND ENGINEERS ARE CONSTANTLY SEEKING TO IMPROVE THE CONTROL MECHANISMS OF AIRCRAFT.

A HIGH PROPORTION OF FLYING ACCIDENTS ARE CAUSED BY INSTABILITY, LEADING TO LOSS OF CONTROL AND STRUCTURAL FAILURE THROUGH OVERLOADING OF FLYING SURFACES.

RAPID REACTION BY THE CONTROLS TO CHANGES IN AIRFLOW IS ESSENTIAL TO STABLE FLIGHT—AND HERE MANY NATURAL SYSTEMS HAVE A CAPABILITY FAR BEYOND OUR TECHNOLOGY.

RECENT RESEARCH HAS SHOWN THAT ONE OF TH[E] MOST REMARKABLY SENSITIVE SYSTEMS FOR CORRECTING ROLL, PITCH, AND YAW IN FLIGHT IS POSSESSED BY THE DESERT LOCUST. . .

MANY ANIMALS POSSESS GRAVITY-SENSITIVE RECEPTORS IN THEIR BODIES, ENABLING THEM TO KNOW WHICH WAY IS "UP", AND THEREFORE MAINTAIN STABILITY.

LOCUSTS LACK SUCH RECEPTORS, BUT CLEARLY POSSESS FLIGHT STABILITY FOR THEIR LONG MIGRATIONS IN SEARCH OF FOOD.

THE BASIS OF THE SYSTEM IS A STURDY "CENTRAL FLIGHT MOTOR" IN THE THORAX—NERVE CENTERS WHICH KEEP THE WINGS BEATING REGULARLY WITHOUT DIRECTION FROM THE BRAIN.

AIRFLOW OVER THE LOCUST HEAD TURNS THE MOTOR ON AND MAINTAINS FLIGHT, CONTACT STIMULATION OF RECEPTORS IN ITS FEET TURNS THE MOTOR OFF WHEN IT LANDS. . .

THREE MOTIONS—YAW, PITCH, AND ROLL—MUST BE CONTROLLED IF A LOCUST IS TO MAINTAIN STABLE FLIGHT.

horizon

IT RESPONDS TO AN INCORRECT ROLL ATTITUDE BY ROTATING ITS HEAD UNTIL ITS EYES ARE ALIGNED PARALLEL TO THE HORIZON, OR UNTIL EACH EYE IS MAXIMALLY STIMULATED BY LIGHT FROM ABOVE

pitch

yaw

roll

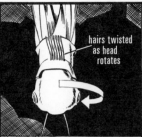

hairs twisted as head rotates

THE SHAFTS OF HAIRS IN THE BACK OF ITS NECK ARE THUS TWISTED BY THE DIFFERENCE IN ANGLE BETWEEN ITS HEAD AND ITS BODY.

THIS TWISTING TRIGGERS RECEPTORS WHICH SIGNAL THE CENTRAL FLIGHT MOTOR TO MODIFY THE WING BEATS IN ORDER TO REALIGN BODY WITH HEAD—AND THUS CORRECT THE ROLL. . .

U.S. RESEARCHERS MOUNTED A LOCUST WITH SOFT WAX IN FRONT OF A MINIATURE WIND TUNNEL, SO THAT IT WAS FREE TO TURN LEFT OR RIGHT.

airflow

IN TOTAL DARKNESS, THE AIRFLOW WAS SWIVELLED 25 DEGREES RIGHT, AS IF THE LOCUST, IN FLIGHT, HAD UNINTENTIONALLY YAWED LEFT.

WITHIN 1/3 SECOND, FOUR REACTIONS OCCURRED: ON EACH DOWNSTROKE THE RIGHT WING TWISTED DOWNWARDS AND THE LEFT UPWARDS; THE ABDOMEN SWUNG RIGHT, LIKE A RUDDER; THE LEGS SWUNG RIGHT; AND THE HEAD ROTATED CLOCKWISE, LIKE THE NOSE OF A PLANE BANKING RIGHT.

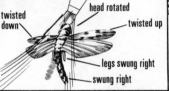

twisted down

head rotated

twisted up

legs swung right

swung right

THE RESULT WAS AN INSTANTANEOUS CORRECTION OF FLIGHT PATH TO MAINTAIN ORIGINAL DIRECTION— BUT WHAT MECHANISM IS RESPONSIBLE FOR SUCH PRECISE CONTROL?

THE TRACING OF NERVE PATHS IN THE LOCUST SHOWS THAT FLIGHT DIRECTION IS MAINTAINED BY SIGNALS FROM A PATCH OF HAIRS ON THE HEAD SENSITIVE TO CHANGES IN WIND FLOW.

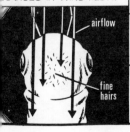

airflow

fine hairs

IF THE RELATIVE WIND FLOW, CREATED BY FORWARD FLIGHT, ALTERS BECAUSE OF ACCIDENTAL YAWING, ROLLING, OR PITCHING, THE HAIRS DETECT IT, AND THE CENTRAL FLIGHT MOTOR MOVES THE CONTROLS: WINGS, ABDOMEN, AND LEGS.

direction of wind flow

yaw

flight path

wings stopped

THIS INGENIOUS AUTOMATIC MECHANISM ONLY WORKS, HOWEVER, DURING FLIGHT; LOCUSTS WHOSE WINGS STOPPED DURING TESTS DID NOT RESPOND TO AIRFLOW CHANGES.

SCIENTISTS ARE STILL INVESTIGATING THE ENORMOUSLY SOPHISTICATED CONTROL SYSTEM OF THAT SIMPLE FLYING MACHINE, THE DESERT LOCUST. . .

The only flying mammal

The hundreds of species of bats in the world show an evo tionary success unmatched by any other mammals: the mastery flight.

TODAY MANKIND IS TAKING A GREATER INTEREST IN THE OTHER LIVING INHABITANTS OF HIS PLANET, WITH INCREASING AWARENESS THAT MAN HIMSELF IS ONLY ONE OF A MYRIAD EQUALLY FASCINATING CREATURES.

MANY ANIMALS HAVE BEEN FOUND TO POSSESS ABILITIES WHICH MAY HELP MAN BETTER UNDERSTAND HIS OWN FACULTIES.

ZOOLOGISTS ALSO STUDY WAYS IN WHICH OTHER CREATURES HAVE ADAPTED THEMSELVES TO THEIR ENVIRONMENT, SEEKING CLUES TO "SURVIVAL ABILITY".

IN THIS FIELD, ONE OF T LEAST KNOWN AND MOST INTERESTING GROUP OF MAMM ARE THE BATS, WHOSE 80C DIFFERENT SPECIES, ALL RELATED TO MAN, HAVE BE REMARKABLY SUCCESSFUL.

MORE THAN 800 SPECIES OF BATS ARE KNOWN, REPRESENTING ONE SEVENTH OF ALL SPECIES OF MAMMALS, OR MORE THAN ANY GROUP EXCEPT THE RODENTS.

THIS EVOLUTIONARY SUCCESS STORY HAS ALL RESULTED FROM A TECHNICAL BREAKTHROUGH WHICH ONLY THE BATS, AMONG MAMMALS, HAS ACHIEVED: SUSTAINED, POWERED FLIGHT.

THE ADVANTAGES OF FLIGHT——IN PROVIDING ESCAPE FROM PREDATORS, A WIDE RANGE OF HABITAT, AND A CHOICE OF DIET—— IS OBVIOUS IN THE ENORMOUS NUMBER OF SPECIES OF BIRDS AND INSECTS.

THE FACT THAT BATS ARI EQUALLY SUCCESSFUL IN DIVERSIFYING HAS BEEN CONCEALED BY THEIR NOCTURN HABITS.

THE ONLY MAMMALS TO ACHIEVE POWERED FLIGHT, BATS HAVE EVOLVED FOUR SIGNIFICANT ADVANTAGES OVER BIRDS AND INSECTS.

FIRST, THEIR WINGS ARE MADE OF SKIN STRETCHED BETWEEN THE "FINGERS" OF THE FORELIMBS, WITH MANY JOINTS, GIVING GREAT MANOEUVRABILITY.

SECOND, THE HIND LIMBS, BEING INCORPORATED INTO THE WING MEMBRANE, HELP IN FLIGHT (BUT CANNOT SUPPORT THE BODY—HENCE BATS MUST HANG WHEN AT REST).

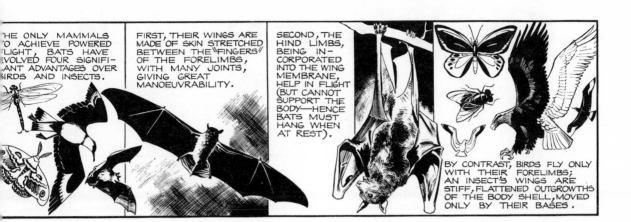

BY CONTRAST, BIRDS FLY ONLY WITH THEIR FORELIMBS; AN INSECT'S WINGS ARE STIFF, FLATTENED OUTGROWTHS OF THE BODY SHELL, MOVED ONLY BY THEIR BASES.

flow

heat loss

blood vessels

THE THIRD DIFFERENCE BETWEEN BATS AND OTHER FLIERS IS THAT THE LARGE SKIN SURFACE OF THE WINGS BECOMES A "RADIATOR" FOR COOLING THE BODY DURING SUSTAINED FLIGHT.

THIS INGENIOUS MECHANISM COULD OVERHEAT IN SUNLIGHT—WHICH PROBABLY EXPLAINS WHY BATS ARE NOCTURNAL.

NIGHT FLYING REQUIRES SPECIAL NAVIGATION AIDS, AND THUS BATS DEVELOPED THEIR FOURTH UNIQUE CAPABILITY: CONTINUOUS ECHO-LOCATION.

IN THIS, BATS HAVE A SYSTEM OF A DEGREE OF SOPHISTICATION AND SENSITIVITY THAT MAN-MADE EQUIPMENT CANNOT MATCH.

WHEN CRUISING, A BAT EMITS CONTINUOUS ULTRASONIC PULSES AT RATES BETWEEN 5 AND 20 PER SECOND; ECHOES OF THESE SOUNDS ENABLES IT TO AVOID OBSTACLES AND LOCATE ITS INSECT PREY.

ONCE PREY IS DETECTED, THE PULSE RATE SPEEDS UP AS MUCH AS TEN TIMES, WHILE THE BAT INTERCEPTS, USING GREAT SPEED AND AGILITY.

SOME INSECTS ESCAPE BY PRODUCING THEIR OWN ULTRASONIC PULSES, WHICH DETER THE PURSUER — PERHAPS BY "JAMMING" ITS ECHOLOCATION EQUIPMENT.

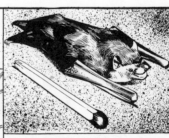

THUS SCIENCE HAS MUCH TO LEARN FROM THE STUDY OF BATS — A SUCCESSFUL GENUS OF 800 SPECIES, RANGING IN SIZE FROM 1·5 METERS TO ONE OF THE SMALLEST MAMMALS KNOWN . . .

Communication between insect.

Animals have many intriguing methods of communication, some insects have evolved amazingly sensitive systems wh depend upon airborne chemical molecules.

THE AMAZING EVOLUTIONARY SUCCESS OF INSECTS —— THEY OUTNUMBER ALL OTHER CREATURES —— IS PARTLY DUE TO THEIR POWERS OF COMMUNICATION.

SOME MALE MOTHS, FOR EXAMPLE, CAN DETECT FEMALES UP TO TWO MILES AWAY —— FAR BEYOND RANGE OF SIGHT OR SOUND.

NATURALISTS LONG BELIEVED THAT THEY COMMUNICATE CHEMICALLY, BUT THE AIRBORNE SIGNALS ARE SO MINUTE THAT THEY DEFIED DETECTION.

TODAY, HIGHLY SENSITIV GAS-ANALYZING TECH-NIQUES ARE DISCOVER ING REMARKABLE CHEMICAL MESSENGER BETWEEN INSECTS.

ENTOMOLOGISTS HAVE NOW ESTABLISHED SEVERAL FUNCTIONS OF CHEMICAL MESSENGERS BETWEEN INSECTS.

ONE GROUP CON-SISTS OF MINUTE TRACES OF POWER-FUL STIMULANTS, DRIFTING THROUGH THE AIR IN SINGLE MOLECULES.

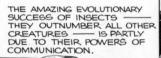

MAN AND OTHER ANIMALS DETECT SIMILAR SUBSTANCES BY SMELL, WHEN THE OLFACTORY CENTERS IN THE NOSE ARE TRIGGERED.

INSECTS DO NOT HAVE NOSES, BUT SOME HAVE REMARKABLY SENSITIVE ANTENNAE FOR DETEC TING CHEMICAL SIGNAL FROM DISTANT SOURCES

AIRBORNE CHEMICAL MESSENGERS BETWEEN INSECTS HAVE SPECIFIC AND IMMEDIATE EFFECTS, EVEN OVER LONG DISTANCES.

ONE IS TO ATTRACT MALES TO FEMALES; THIS IS OBVIOUSLY IMPORTANT FOR NIGHT-FLYING INSECTS LIKE MOTHS.

IN SOME INSECTS, THE FEMALES HAVE LOST THEIR WINGS DURING EVOLUTION, BECOMING IMMOBILE "EGG-FACTORIES", DEPENDENT UPON BEING FOUND BY THE MALES.

MALES CAN DETECT 1 PART IN 1,000,000,000,000,000,000 OF THE FEMALE SEX LURE, BY THEIR INCREDIBLY SENSITIVE ANTENNAE.

ENTOMOLOGISTS FIND THE HIGHEST DEVELOPMENT OF CHEMICAL COMMUNICATION BETWEEN THE "SOCIAL" INSECTS : BEES, ANTS, WASPS, TERMITES.

THIS SYSTEM ENABLES MASSES OF SUCH INSECTS TO BEHAVE ALMOST LIKE A SINGLE ORGANISM, WITH INDIVIDUALS REPRESENTING "CELLS."

THE QUEEN BEE PRODUCES HIGHLY IMPORTANT CHEMICALS, WHICH ARE PASSED ON BY TOUCH FROM BEE TO BEE THROUGHOUT THE HIVE.

ONE USE OF THE QUEEN SUBSTANCE IS TO ATTRACT MALES DURING THE MATING FLIGHT —— BUT THERE IS AN EVEN MORE REMARKABLE FUNCTION.

THE MOST IMPORTANT FUNCTION OF THE QUEEN'S CHEMICAL MESSENGER IS TO 'GOVERN' THE HIVE ; WHEN PRESENT, IT PREVENTS WORKER BEES FROM BUILDING THE SPECIAL CELLS WHICH PRODUCE NEW QUEENS.

THIS ENSURES THE PRIMACY OF A SINGLE QUEEN; IF THE "MESSENGER LEVEL" FALLS (BECAUSE SHE BECOMES WEAK, OR LEAVES THE HIVE WITH A SWARM), NEW QUEENS ARE QUICKLY BRED.

OTHER INSECTS USE SUCH CHEMICALS TO IDENTIFY FOOD SOURCES, LAY FORAGE TRAILS, AND GIVE ALARM SIGNALS.

INCREASING KNOWLEDGE OF SUCH SOPHISTICATED SYSTEMS MAY HELP SCIENCE IN PEST CONTROL —— THE ENDLESS STRUGGLE BETWEEN MAN AND INSECT.

A new way of seeing

In one of the most extraordinary manifestations of the adaptive potential of the brain, a totally blind animal has learned to see again.

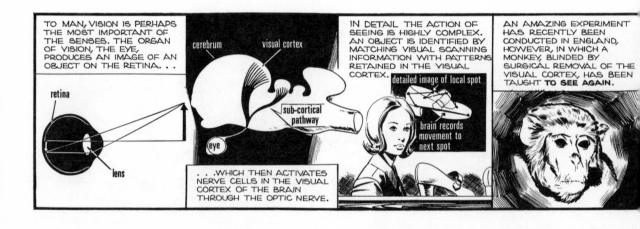

TO MAN, VISION IS PERHAPS THE MOST IMPORTANT OF THE SENSES. THE ORGAN OF VISION, THE EYE, PRODUCES AN IMAGE OF AN OBJECT ON THE RETINA. . .

retina

lens

cerebrum

visual cortex

sub-cortical pathway

eye

. . .WHICH THEN ACTIVATES NERVE CELLS IN THE VISUAL CORTEX OF THE BRAIN THROUGH THE OPTIC NERVE.

IN DETAIL THE ACTION OF SEEING IS HIGHLY COMPLEX. AN OBJECT IS IDENTIFIED BY MATCHING VISUAL SCANNING INFORMATION WITH PATTERNS RETAINED IN THE VISUAL CORTEX.

detailed image of local spot

brain records movement to next spot

AN AMAZING EXPERIMENT HAS RECENTLY BEEN CONDUCTED IN ENGLAND, HOWEVER, IN WHICH A MONKEY, BLINDED BY SURGICAL REMOVAL OF THE VISUAL CORTEX, HAS BEEN TAUGHT **TO SEE AGAIN.**

IT IS KNOWN THAT WE RECOGNIZE OBJECTS THROUGH A PROCESS WHICH PSYCHOLOGISTS HAVE TERMED 'FEATURE ANALYSIS'.

scan path

RECENT EXPERIMENTS ON THE ACTION OF 'SEEING' INDICATE THAT OUR EYES FOCUS ON SPECIFIC SPOTS ON AN OBJECT IN TURN, AND JUMP FROM ONE SPOT TO ANOTHER, CREATING WHAT HAS BEEN CALLED A 'SCAN PATH'.

THE VISUAL CORTEX CONSISTS OF INDIVIDUAL NERVE CELLS WHICH SOMEHOW RETAIN THE INTERNAL PATTERNS OF RECOGNIZABLE OBJECTS.

object identified by matching scan path with information in visual cortex

visual cortex

IN RECENT YEARS SCIENTISTS IN ENGLAND HAVE MADE SIGNIFICANT PROGRESS WITH FURTHER STUDIES OF THE MECHANISM OF SIGHT. ONE AMAZING EXPERIMENT HAS BEEN CONDUCTED BY DR. NICHOLAS HUMPHREY OF THE DEPARTMENT OF ANIMAL BEHAVIOR AT CAMBRIDGE UNIVERSITY.

IN AN OPERATION PERFORMED IN THE PSYCHOLOGICAL LABORATORY IN CAMBRIDGE, A FEMALE MONKEY—KNOWN AS HELEN—HAD HER VISUAL CORTEX COMPLETELY REMOVED.

FOLLOWING THE OPERATION HELEN APPEARED TO BE COMPLETELY BLIND AND HAD TO BE APPROPRIATELY CARED FOR.

AFTER SEVERAL YEARS OF CAREFUL TRAINING, HOWEVER, HELEN HAS BEEN TAUGHT TO SEE AGAIN—BUT IN A WAY COMPLETELY DIFFERENT FROM NORMAL SEEING.

AT THE UNIVERSITY OF CAMBRIDGE, ENGLAND, THE BLINDED MONKEY HELEN WAS CONTINUALLY URGED BY TRAINING TO ATTEMPT TO SEE AGAIN.

THE MONKEY'S SIGHT GRADUALLY REDEVELOPED, BY THE BRAIN LEARNING TO INTERPRET INFORMATION COMING FROM THE EYE THROUGH THE "FALL-BACK" SUB-CORTICAL PATHWAY.

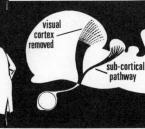

visual cortex removed

sub-cortical pathway

AFTER SEVERAL YEARS OF HER SIGHT REDEVELOPING, HELEN CAN NOW SAFELY RUN THROUGH THE WOODS NEAR CAMBRIDGE. . .

. . .AND CAN MOVE RAPIDLY AND ACCURATELY TO PICK UP SUCH SMALL ITEMS OF FOOD AS CURRANTS THROWN AT RANDOM.

A MAJOR DISADVANTAGE IN THE PRESENT SIGHT OF THE EXPERIMENTAL MONKEY HELEN IS THAT SHE HAS NO "FEATURE ANALYSIS," BECAUSE OF THE REMOVAL OF HER VISUAL CORTEX. HELEN CAN "SEE" AN OBJECT. . .

matching scan path removed with visual cortex

. . .BUT IN THE ABSENCE OF A BANK OF INTERNAL SYMBOLS IN THE MEMORY SYSTEM SHE CANNOT IDENTIFY AN OBJECT IN TERMS OF PAST EXPERIENCES.

NEVERTHELESS, THE FACT THAT THE MONKEY'S SIGHT HAS REDEVELOPED USING THE SUB-CORTICAL PATHWAY IS A VAST IMPROVEMENT OVER COMPLETE BLINDNESS.

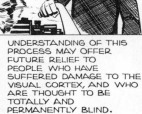

UNDERSTANDING OF THIS PROCESS MAY OFFER FUTURE RELIEF TO PEOPLE WHO HAVE SUFFERED DAMAGE TO THE VISUAL CORTEX, AND WHO ARE THOUGHT TO BE TOTALLY AND PERMANENTLY BLIND.

Despite their reputation, some birds exhibit a faster learni
capacity than supposedly more intelligent animals, such as monke
and cats.

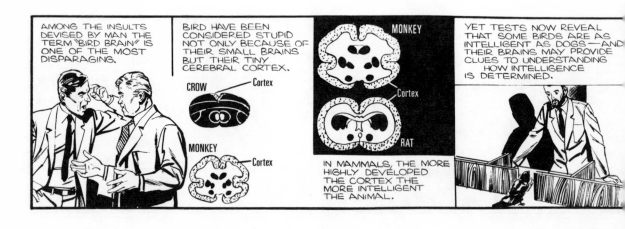

AMONG THE INSULTS DEVISED BY MAN THE TERM "BIRD BRAIN" IS ONE OF THE MOST DISPARAGING.

BIRD HAVE BEEN CONSIDERED STUPID NOT ONLY BECAUSE OF THEIR SMALL BRAINS BUT THEIR TINY CEREBRAL CORTEX.

CROW — Cortex

MONKEY — Cortex

MONKEY
Cortex
RAT

IN MAMMALS, THE MORE HIGHLY DEVELOPED THE CORTEX THE MORE INTELLIGENT THE ANIMAL.

YET TESTS NOW REVEAL THAT SOME BIRDS ARE AS INTELLIGENT AS DOGS—AND THEIR BRAINS MAY PROVIDE CLUES TO UNDERSTANDING HOW INTELLIGENCE IS DETERMINED.

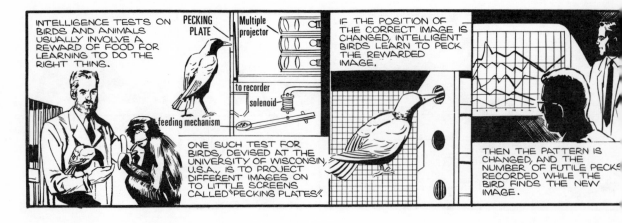

INTELLIGENCE TESTS ON BIRDS AND ANIMALS USUALLY INVOLVE A REWARD OF FOOD FOR LEARNING TO DO THE RIGHT THING.

PECKING PLATE

Multiple projector

to recorder
solenoid
feeding mechanism

ONE SUCH TEST FOR BIRDS, DEVISED AT THE UNIVERSITY OF WISCONSIN, U.S.A., IS TO PROJECT DIFFERENT IMAGES ON TO LITTLE SCREENS CALLED "PECKING PLATES".

IF THE POSITION OF THE CORRECT IMAGE IS CHANGED, INTELLIGENT BIRDS LEARN TO PECK THE REWARDED IMAGE.

THEN THE PATTERN IS CHANGED, AND THE NUMBER OF FUTILE PECKS RECORDED WHILE THE BIRD FINDS THE NEW IMAGE.

AN OUTSTANDING FEAT OF INTELLIGENT BIRDS SUCH AS CROWS IS TO RECOGNIZE "SETS". THEY CAN PICK OUT AN ODD IMAGE EVEN THOUGH THEY MAY NEVER HAVE SEEN THE ACTUAL SHAPES BEFORE.

THE IMAGES ON THE PECKING PLATES CAN BE MIXED UP IN ANY ORDER, WITH THE ODD ONE ALWAYS BEING REWARDED—AND THE CROW PICKS IT.

reward
1
reward
2
reward
3

IN SUCH A TEST A CROW IS FAR SUPERIOR TO THE CAT, AND EVEN BETTER THAN THE MONKEY.

A CROW LEARNS TO PECK THE ODD IMAGE EVEN FROM PICTURES, WHATEVER THEIR ORDER.

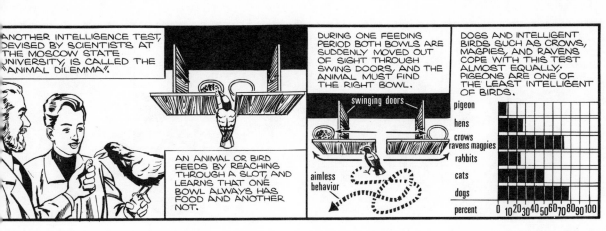

ANOTHER INTELLIGENCE TEST, DEVISED BY SCIENTISTS AT THE MOSCOW STATE UNIVERSITY, IS CALLED THE "ANIMAL DILEMMA".

AN ANIMAL OR BIRD FEEDS BY REACHING THROUGH A SLOT, AND LEARNS THAT ONE BOWL ALWAYS HAS FOOD AND ANOTHER NOT.

DURING ONE FEEDING PERIOD BOTH BOWLS ARE SUDDENLY MOVED OUT OF SIGHT THROUGH SWING DOORS, AND THE ANIMAL MUST FIND THE RIGHT BOWL.

swinging doors

aimless behavior

DOGS AND INTELLIGENT BIRDS SUCH AS CROWS, MAGPIES, AND RAVENS COPE WITH THIS TEST ALMOST EQUALLY; PIGEONS ARE ONE OF THE LEAST INTELLIGENT OF BIRDS.

pigeon
hens
crows ravens magpies
rabbits
cats
dogs
percent   0 10 20 30 40 50 60 70 80 90 100

IN EXPERIMENTS IN WHICH A BIRD'S CORTEX IS REMOVED OR IMPAIRED, THE INTELLIGENCE SEEMS LITTLE CHANGED.

IT NOW APPEARS THAT, UNLIKE MAMMALS, THE INTELLIGENCE CENTERS OF BIRD BRAINS ARE IN THE HYPERSTRIATUM RATHER THAN THE CORTEX.

CROW
Cortex
Hyperstriatum (intelligence)
MONKEY
Cortex (intelligence)

SCIENTISTS BELIEVE THAT THE FUNCTION OF THE BIRD'S HYPERSTRIATUM WILL BE MORE SIMPLE TO UNRAVEL THAN THE CORTEX OF MAMMALS...

...AND THAT STUDIES OF "BIRD BRAINS" MAY PROVIDE A KEY TO UNDERSTANDING HOW BRAINS WORK—A VITAL FACTOR IN THE BUILDING OF "INTELLIGENT" COMPUTERS.

Communicating with chimpanzees

One of the major barriers to inter-species communication — the inability of animals other than man to use speech—may be overcome by sign language.

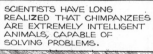

SCIENTISTS HAVE LONG REALIZED THAT CHIMPANZEES ARE EXTREMELY INTELLIGENT ANIMALS, CAPABLE OF SOLVING PROBLEMS.

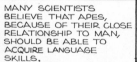

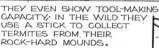

THEY EVEN SHOW TOOL-MAKING CAPACITY: IN THE WILD THEY USE A STICK TO COLLECT TERMITES FROM THEIR ROCK-HARD MOUNDS.

COMMUNICATION BETWEEN APE AND MAN HAS PROVED DIFFICULT, HOWEVER, BECAUSE THEIR PHYSIOLOGY DOES NOT ENABLE THEM TO LEARN SPOKEN LANGUAGES.

NOW A MAJOR BREAKTHROUGH HAS BEEN ACHIEVED BY U.S. SCIENTISTS, WHO HAVE TAUGHT A CHIMPANZEE TO COMMUNICATE BY SIGN LANGUAGE. . .

MANY SCIENTISTS BELIEVE THAT APES, BECAUSE OF THEIR CLOSE RELATIONSHIP TO MAN, SHOULD BE ABLE TO ACQUIRE LANGUAGE SKILLS.

DIFFERENCES IN THE CHIMPANZEE'S CENTRAL NERVOUS SYSTEM HAVE, HOWEVER, FRUSTRATED ALL ATTEMPTS TO TEACH THEM VOCAL SPEECH.

IN 1966 TWO PSYCHOLOGISTS AT THE UNIVERSITY OF NEVADA, DRS. BEATRICE AND ALLEN GARDNER, ADOPTED A NEW APPROACH WITH AN 8-MONTH-OLD CHIMPANZEE NAMED WASHOE.

THEY DECIDED TO BRING UP WASHOE IN A HUMAN ENVIRONMENT—IN WHICH ONLY **SIGN** LANGUAGE WOULD BE USED, EVEN BY HUMANS.

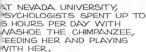
AT NEVADA UNIVERSITY, PSYCHOLOGISTS SPENT UP TO 5 HOURS PER DAY WITH WASHOE THE CHIMPANZEE, FEEDING HER AND PLAYING WITH HER.

WITHIN A YEAR, WASHOE HAD LEARNED SCORES OF SIGNS FOR VARIOUS ACTIVITIES. MORE IMPORTANTLY, SHE COULD LINK THEM INTO EXPRESSIONS.

IF SHE WANTED WATER, SHE MADE THE "DRINK" SIGN. IF A COLA, SHE PREFACED IT WITH THE SIGNS FOR "GIVE ME" AND "SWEET".

THEY USED ONLY THE STANDARD DEAF-AND-DUMB SIGN LANGUAGE, NOT ONLY WITH WASHOE, BUT WITH EACH OTHER.

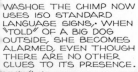
WASHOE THE CHIMP NOW USES 150 STANDARD LANGUAGE SIGNS. WHEN "TOLD" OF A BIG DOG OUTSIDE, SHE BECOMES ALARMED, EVEN THOUGH THERE ARE NO OTHER CLUES TO ITS PRESENCE.

EVENTUALLY WASHOE WAS MOVED FROM NEVADA TO OKLAHOMA UNIVERSITY, TO JOIN 25 OTHER CHIMPANZEES UNDERGOING SIMILAR SIGN LANGUAGE TRAINING.

SCIENTISTS ARE NOW WATCHING HOPEFULLY FOR SOME EXCHANGE OF SIGNS BETWEEN THE ANIMALS, AS WELL AS WITH THEIR HUMAN TEACHERS.

IF THEN ASKED IF SHE WANTS TO GO OUTSIDE AND PLAY—HER FAVORITE ACTIVITY— WASHOE VIGOROUSLY REPLIES "NO".

HAVING TRAINED WASHOE TO USE SIGN LANGUAGE (INSTEAD OF SPEECH), U.S. PSYCHOLOGISTS EAGERLY AWAITED HER ARRIVAL AT SEXUAL MATURITY.

SUCH AN EVENT WOULD BE HIGHLY SIGNIFICANT, SINCE MANY ANTHROPOLOGISTS BELIEVE THAT MAN FIRST COMMUNICATED BY SIGNS.

WHEN SHE HAS OFFSPRING, WILL SHE TEACH THEM THE SIGNS THAT SHE NOW USES SO FLUENTLY, THUS PASSING ON HER ACQUIRED "LANGUAGE"?

ONLY LATER, PERHAPS, DID HE MAKE THE EVOLUTIONARY ADVANCE THAT LED TO TRUE SPEECH AND SINGLED HIM OUT FROM OTHER PRIMATES. . .

Return to life

One of the processes in life which science still cannot expla[in] is the ability of some tiny animals to revive from a state which, [in] ordinary biological terms, represents death.

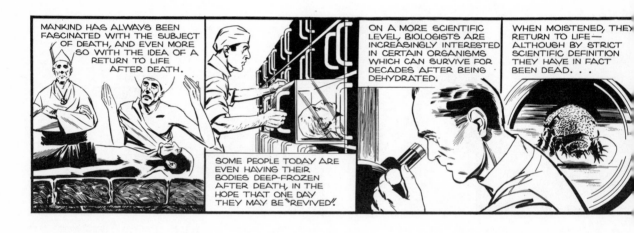

MANKIND HAS ALWAYS BEEN FASCINATED WITH THE SUBJECT OF DEATH, AND EVEN MORE SO WITH THE IDEA OF A RETURN TO LIFE AFTER DEATH.

SOME PEOPLE TODAY ARE EVEN HAVING THEIR BODIES DEEP-FROZEN AFTER DEATH, IN THE HOPE THAT ONE DAY THEY MAY BE "REVIVED".

ON A MORE SCIENTIFIC LEVEL, BIOLOGISTS ARE INCREASINGLY INTERESTED IN CERTAIN ORGANISMS WHICH CAN SURVIVE FOR DECADES AFTER BEING DEHYDRATED.

WHEN MOISTENED, THEY RETURN TO LIFE— ALTHOUGH BY STRICT SCIENTIFIC DEFINITION THEY HAVE IN FACT BEEN DEAD. . .

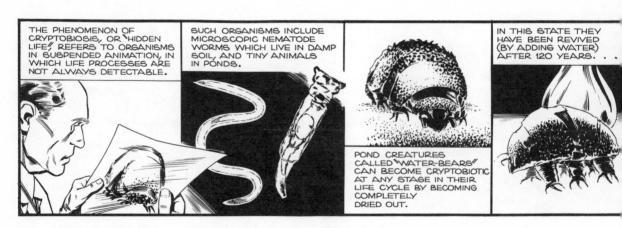

THE PHENOMENON OF CRYPTOBIOSIS, OR "HIDDEN LIFE", REFERS TO ORGANISMS IN SUSPENDED ANIMATION, IN WHICH LIFE PROCESSES ARE NOT ALWAYS DETECTABLE.

SUCH ORGANISMS INCLUDE MICROSCOPIC NEMATODE WORMS WHICH LIVE IN DAMP SOIL, AND TINY ANIMALS IN PONDS.

POND CREATURES CALLED "WATER-BEARS" CAN BECOME CRYPTOBIOTIC AT ANY STAGE IN THEIR LIFE CYCLE BY BECOMING COMPLETELY DRIED OUT.

IN THIS STATE THEY HAVE BEEN REVIVED (BY ADDING WATER) AFTER 120 YEARS. . .

CRYPTOBIOTIC ANIMALS EXHIBIT PHENOMENAL RESISTANCE TO CONDITIONS THAT WOULD BE INSTANTLY FATAL IF THEY WERE NORMALLY ACTIVE.

X-RAYS 570,000 roentgens

THE DOSE NEEDED TO PRODUCE THE SAME EFFECT IN HUMANS IS BARELY 500 ROENTGENS...

X-RAYS 500 roentgens

"WATER-BEARS" HAVE SURVIVED 150 DEG. CELSIUS —FAR ABOVE THE BOILING POINT OF WATER—AND ALSO LONG PERIODS AT 0·008 KELVIN, CLOSE TO ABSOLUTE ZERO.

THEY ALSO RESIST RADIATION; THE X-RAY EXPOSURE REQUIRED TO KILL 50% OF THOSE EXPOSED WITHIN 24 HOURS WAS A STAGGERING 570,000 ROENTGENS.

THIS CHALLENGES THE LONG-STANDING BIOLOGICAL ARGUMENT THAT WATER IS ESSENTIAL TO LIFE, BY MAINTAINING THE THREE-DIMENSIONAL STRUCTURE OF MOLECULES SUCH AS PROTEINS.

CRYPTOBIOTIC ANIMALS SEEM TO BE ABLE TO MAINTAIN THE SHAPE OF THEIR MOLECULES BY OTHER MEANS UNTIL WATER IS ADDED AGAIN.

STUDIES OF NEMATODE WORMS DURING CRYPTOBIOSIS SHOW THAT THE ANIMALS HAVE LOST LITERALLY ALL THE WATER FROM THEIR CELLS.

THIS ABILITY TO SURVIVE TOTAL DESICCATION— WHICH NORMALLY KILLS ALL LIVING SYSTEMS— AT PRESENT DEFIES BIOLOGICAL EXPLANATION.

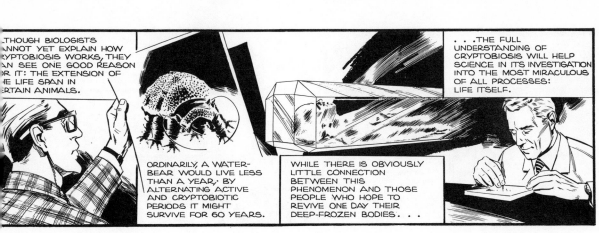

ALTHOUGH BIOLOGISTS CANNOT YET EXPLAIN HOW CRYPTOBIOSIS WORKS, THEY CAN SEE ONE GOOD REASON FOR IT: THE EXTENSION OF THE LIFE SPAN IN CERTAIN ANIMALS.

...THE FULL UNDERSTANDING OF CRYPTOBIOSIS WILL HELP SCIENCE IN ITS INVESTIGATION INTO THE MOST MIRACULOUS OF ALL PROCESSES: LIFE ITSELF.

ORDINARILY, A WATER-BEAR WOULD LIVE LESS THAN A YEAR; BY ALTERNATING ACTIVE AND CRYPTOBIOTIC PERIODS IT MIGHT SURVIVE FOR 60 YEARS.

WHILE THERE IS OBVIOUSLY LITTLE CONNECTION BETWEEN THIS PHENOMENON AND THOSE PEOPLE WHO HOPE TO REVIVE ONE DAY THEIR DEEP-FROZEN BODIES...

Mysteries of animal orientatio

Among the many capabilities exhibited by other animals
man cannot emulate or duplicate technologically is the sens
orientation.

STUDIES OF ANIMAL BEHAVIOR ARE TODAY YIELDING NEW AND REMARKABLE KNOWLEDGE, OF GREAT INTEREST TO HUMAN PHYSIOLOGISTS.

ONE OF THE GREAT MYSTERIES OF THE ANIMAL KINGDOM IS THE UNCANNY ABILITY OF WILD CREATURES TO FIND THEIR WAY ACROSS VAST DISTANCES.

SCIENTISTS ARE STILL TRYING TO UNDERSTAND WHY MAN SHOULD BE SO INFERIOR TO MANY ANIMALS IN THIS SENSE OF ORIENTATION.

RECENT RESEARCH (BEES, FOR EXAMPLE, SUGGESTS THAT THEY ACTUALLY TAKE CROSS BEARINGS ON LANDMAR JUST AS NAVIGATORS D

THE REMARKABLE NAVIGATIONAL ABILITY OF BEES FIRST CAME TO LIGHT DURING RESEARCH IN GERMANY INTO THEIR MATING PATTERNS.

PROF. RUTTNER, A BIOLOGIST, WANTED TO OBSERVE THE MATING FLIGHT OF THE QUEEN BEE AND THE MALE DRONES.

BY TYING A SMALL BALLOON TO THE QUEEN, HE FOUND THAT SHE INVARIABLY WENT TO AN AREA SOME MILES FROM THE HIVE.

THIS AREA MEASURED A FEW HUNDRED YARDS SQUA — AND DRONES WOULD ONL MATE WITH HER INSIDE TH AREA. BUT HOW DID THEY FIND IT?

THE GREAT PUZZLE ABOUT THE BEES' MATING AREA IS HOW THEY RETURN TO IT EACH YEAR. THE QUEEN, WHICH LIVES SEVERAL YEARS, COULD REMEMBER IT . . .

. . . BUT DRONES DIE IN THEIR FIRST WINTER. EACH NEW GENERATION, THEREFORE, MUST FIND ITS WAY TO THE MATING AREA, WITHOUT GUIDES.

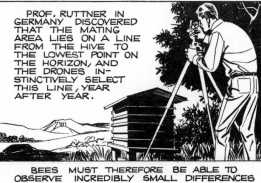

PROF. RUTTNER IN GERMANY DISCOVERED THAT THE MATING AREA LIES ON A LINE FROM THE HIVE TO THE LOWEST POINT ON THE HORIZON, AND THE DRONES IN-STINCTIVELY SELECT THIS LINE, YEAR AFTER YEAR.

BEES MUST THEREFORE BE ABLE TO OBSERVE INCREDIBLY SMALL DIFFERENCES IN ANGLE . . .

CAN THE BEE'S COMPOUND EYE DETECT THE TINY CHANGES IN ANGLE THAT THEIR UNCANNY NAVIGATION SEEMS TO DEPEND UPON?

AN ENGLISH ZOOLOGIST, HORRIDGE, FOUND THAT CRABS (WITH STRUCTURALLY SIMILAR EYES) REACT WHEN THE OBJECT THEY ARE WATCHING MOVES THROUGH ONLY SIX SECONDS OF ARC.

FOR COMPARISON, THE ANGLE AT WHICH WE SEE THE SUN IS 300 TIMES AS LARGE.

SUN

6 SECS. OF ARC = 1/300 OF THIS ANGLE

CRABS DETECT THE SUN'S MOVEMENT THROUGH ONLY 10 SECONDS OF ARC. (WE NEED A LARGE FIXED TELESCOPE). THE BEE'S EYE SEEMS EQUALLY PERCEPTIVE OF CONTOUR CHANGES . . .

EVIDENCE OF BEES' "CONTOUR NAVIGATION" CAME WHEN A GERMAN SCIENTIST ATTRACTED THEM TO A FEEDING TABLE, THEN CONCEAL-ED THE HIVE, AND FINALLY MOVED THE TABLE WITH THE BEES ON IT.

TABLE MOVED (WITH BEES)

BEES' COURSE TO FEEDING TABLE

HIVE CONCEALED

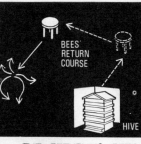

BEES' RETURN COURSE

HIVE

THE RETURNING BEES REVERSED COURSE 180 DEGREES, AS USUAL, TO RETURN HOME— BUT OBVIOUSLY REACHED THE WRONG PLACE.

AFTER FLYING IN RANDOM ZIGZAGS, HOWEVER, THEY LOCATED THEIR HIDDEN HIVE— APPARENTLY BY CORRE-LATING ANGULAR BEARINGS ON HORIZON LANDMARKS, PRESUMABLY OBSERVED AND REMEM-BERED AS THEY LEFT THE HIVE.

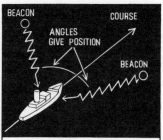

BEACON

COURSE

ANGLES GIVE POSITION

BEACON

THIS IS PRECISELY THE METHOD USED BY SHIPS AND AIRCRAFT TO LOCATE THEMSELVES BY RADIO BEACONS . . . BUT BEES NEED NO INSTRUMENTS . . .

Bird migration puzzle

Scientists investigating the uncanny ability of birds to find th￼
way home continue to find new and unsuspected aspects to ￼
faculty.

SCIENTISTS HAVE LONG ATTEMPTED TO UNDERSTAND HOW EELS, SALMON, WHALES, TURTLES, AND BIRDS—AND EVEN INSECTS—MIGRATE OVER VERY LONG DISTANCES.

MOST SPECTACULARLY, THE ARCTIC TERN FLIES 11,000 MILES EVERY YEAR FROM THE ARCTIC TO THE ANTARCTIC, AND THEN BACK.

SIMILARLY, THE TASMANIAN MUTTONBIRD WINTERS NEAR ALASKA, BUT RETURNS EVERY SPRING TO THE SAME BURROW IN BASS STRAIT TO BREED.

RECENT U.S. ATTEMPTS TO INTERFERE EXPERIMENTAL WITH THIS CAPABILITY HA HOWEVER, LEFT THE EXPERIMENTERS MORE CONFUSED THAN THE BIRDS. . .

THE FACT THAT MOST BIRDS MIGRATE AT NIGHT SUGGESTS THAT THEY MAY USE THE STARS FOR NAVIGATION—BUT MIGRATION INVOLVES MORE THAN JUST KNOWING WHICH IS NORTH OR SOUTH.

BIRDS BLOWN OFF COURSE OR CUT OFF FROM THE STARS BY CLOUDS MUST POSSESS A "MAP" SENSE THAT TELLS THEM WHERE THEY ARE, RELATIVE TO THEIR DESTINATION.

RESEARCH HAS PROVED THAT WHEN DENIED A CLUE SUCH AS THE STARS, BIRDS CAN SWITCH TO OTHER NAVIGATION SYSTEMS.

SCIENTISTS AT NEW YORK STATE UNIVERSITY HAVE RECENTLY PERFORMED A SERIES OF INGENIOUS EXPERIMENTS AIMED AT SOLVING THIS MYSTERY.

SCIENTISTS ERIMENTED EXTENSIVELY H HOMING PIGEONS, AUSE OF THEIR RENOWNED GATIONAL ABILITIES.

'THEY HAVE THE SAME REMARKABLE "MAP SENSE" AS A MIGRATING BIRD BLOWN OFF COURSE, THAT IS, IN TOTALLY STRANGE TERRITORY THEY UNERRINGLY FIND THEIR WAY HOME.

TO FIND OUT EXACTLY WHAT COURSE THEY TAKE, PIGEONS WERE EQUIPPED WITH RADIO TRANSMITTERS, AND FOLLOWED BY AN AIRCRAFT WITH DETECTION APPARATUS.

ATTEMPTS WERE THEN MADE TO CONFUSE THE BIRDS BY VARIOUS MEANS, TO SEE IF THE BASIS OF THEIR "MAP SENSE" COULD BE ISOLATED.

ATTEMPTS TO CONFUSE MING PIGEONS INCLUDED ING THEM WITH TACT. LENSES, WHICH BLED THEM TO SEE Y VERY LARGE, CLOSE ECTS, (BUT NOT AILS OF TERRAIN).

IN CASE THEY OBSERVE THE SUN'S ANGLE ABOVE THE HORIZON TO MEMORIZE THEIR HOME LOFT'S LOCATION, MIRRORS WERE USED TO CHANGE THE **APPARENT** POSITION OF THE SUN.

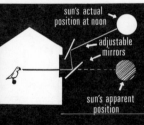

sun's actual position at noon

← adjustable mirrors

sun's apparent position

THIS SHOULD MAKE A PIGEON BELIEVE THAT THE LOFT HAS BEEN SHIFTED NORTH, AND WHEN RELEASED ELSEWHERE IT **SHOULD** FLY TO THE LOFT'S "APPARENT" POSITION.

IN ALL THE CASES MENTIONED BEFORE, HOWEVER, THE RELEASED PIGEONS SIMPLY FLEW STRAIGHT HOME— SOME FROM 250 MILES AWAY, AND ALL ACROSS STRANGE TERRITORY.

E PROMISING EXPERIMENT H PIGEONS INVOLVED TING THEM WITH ECTRICAL COILS WHICH T UP A MAGNETIC FIELD OUND THEIR HEADS.

WITH BOTH SUN AND STARS OBSCURED, TWO GROUPS FROM THE SAME LOFT WERE RELEASED, ONE WITH THE NORTH POLE OF THE FIELD TOWARDS THE HEAD, THE OTHER REVERSED.

SIGNIFICANTLY, ONE GROUP FLEW EASTWARDS STRAIGHT TO THE LOFT, WHILE THE OTHER GROUP FLEW IN AN ALMOST EXACTLY OPPOSITE DIRECTION . . .

. . .WHILE THIS SUGGESTS THAT BIRD MAY USE THE EARTH'S MAGNETIC FIELD FOR MAINTAINING DIRECTION, IT STILL DOES NOT EXPLAIN THEIR "MAP SENSE" WHICH TELLS THEM **WHERE** THEY ARE IN RELATION TO THEIR DESTINATION . . .

New bird migration mysterie

Besides their apparent ability to navigate by the stars and sun, some birds can anticipate seasonal changes.

TODAY MANY COMMERCIAL AIRLINERS USE "INERTIAL NAVIGATION", WHICH SENSES THEIR MOVEMENTS IN RELATION TO THE EARTH.

THIS ENABLES AN AIRCRAFT, WITHOUT REFERENCE TO STARS OR TERRAIN, TO FLY MANY THOUSANDS OF MILES AND KNOW ITS POSITION TO WITHIN ABOUT 10 MILES.

NO MAN-MADE DEVICE CAN YET COMPETE, HOWEVER, WITH THE UNCANNY NAVIGATIONAL INSTINCT OF MIGRATING BIRDS.

NEW RESEARCH HAS DISCLOSED A MORE REMARKABLE BIOLOGI[CAL] MECHANISM THAN EVE[R] THEIR LONG-SUSPECTE[D] ABILITY TO FLY BY THE STARS.

SCIENTISTS HAVE LONG BELIEVED THAT BIRDS NAVIGATE BY STAR PATTERNS —— BUT A SCIENTIST AT CORNELL UNIVERSITY HAS PROVED THAT SOMETHING ELSE IS INVOLVED.

ORNITHOLOGIST STEPHEN EMLEN USED THE INDIGO BUNTING, A SMALL SONG-BIRD THAT ANNUALLY MAKES PRODIGIOUS FLIGHTS BETWEEN CANADA AND CENTRAL AMERICA.

EMLEN RELEASED BUNTINGS INSIDE A PLANETARIUM IN WHICH HE PROJECTED AUTUMN STAR PATTERNS —— WHICH SHOULD HAVE CAUSED THEM TO FLY SOUTH.

SURPRISINGLY, THEY IGNORED THE STARS, AN[D] IN REPEATED EXPERIME[NTS] INVARIABLY HEADED NOR[TH] —— BECAUSE OUTSIDE THE PLANETARIUM IT WAS SPRING....

CORNELL ORNITHOLOGIST EMLEN TRIED TO DISCOVER WHY MIGRATING BIRDS CONSISTENTLY IGNORED STARS IN A PLANETARIUM WHICH CONFLICTED WITH THE REAL SEASON OUTSIDE.

SOME BIOLOGICAL MECHANISM WAS OBVIOUSLY OVER-RIDING THE INSTRUCTIONS PROVIDED BY THE STAR PATTERNS.

IN SPRING, EMLEN BEGAN EXPOSING BIRDS TO PERIODS OF SIMULATED DAYLIGHT THAT LENGTHENED FASTER THAN NATURAL DAYS.

WITHIN A FEW WEEKS, HE ADVANCED THEIR "BIOLOGICAL CLOCKS" BY SIX MONTHS; THEY BEGAN TO SHOW PHYSIOLOGICAL PREPARATIONS FOR AUTUMN MIGRATION...

THE REFUSAL OF MIGRATING BIRDS TO FOLLOW SPRING STAR PATTERNS IN A PLANETARIUM, WHEN THEY KNEW THAT IT WAS AUTUMN...

... PUZZLED CORNELL ORNITHOLOGIST STEPHEN EMLEN, UNTIL HE TRIED REMOVING THE NORTH STAR FROM THE PLANETARIUM SKY.

LACKING THE NORTH STAR, THE BIRDS WERE HOPELESSLY CONFUSED. WHEN IT WAS VISIBLE — AS IT ALWAYS IS IN THE NORTHERN HEMISPHERE — THEY IGNORED THE "FALSE" STAR PATTERNS.

EMLEN CONCLUDED THAT THE BIRDS USE THE POLE STAR FOR BOTH NORTH AND SOUTH JOURNEYS — BUT WHAT TELLS THEM WHEN TO FLY WHICH WAY?

CLEARLY, IF BIRDS USE THE NORTH STAR FOR BOTH NORTH AND SOUTH MIGRATIONS, SOMETHING MUST TELL THEM WHEN TO HEAD AWAY FROM IT OR TOWARDS IT.

CORNELL ORNITHOLOGIST EMLEN BELIEVES THAT THEIR BODY CHEMISTRY TELLS THEM NOT ONLY WHEN TO MIGRATE, BUT IN WHICH DIRECTION.

THE KEY AGENT, HE THINKS, COULD BE A HORMONE, SECRETED IN RESPONSE TO VARYING DAYLIGHT HOURS AS THE SEASONS CHANGE.

THUS THE REMARKABLE NAVIGATIONAL ABILITY OF MIGRATING BIRDS IS NOW SEEN TO INVOLVE EVEN MORE SUBTLE BIOLOGICAL MECHANISMS THAN HUMAN TECHNOLOGY HAS YET ENVISAGED...

Fish migration by temperatur

Some species of fish are capable of regular and extens migrations, without access to the heavenly navigational a apparently used by birds.

THE MIGRATION HABITS OF MANY ANIMALS INVOLVE NAVIGATIONAL ABILITIES THAT SCIENCE STILL CANNOT FULLY EXPLAIN OR DUPLICATE.

SOME BIRDS APPARENTLY NAVIGATE BY THE STARS— BUT THEY CAN ALSO FIND THEIR WAY UNERRINGLY EVEN IN TOTAL CLOUD OVERCAST.

FISH MIGRATIONS ARE EVEN MORE MYSTIFYING, SINCE FISH CANNOT USE CELESTIAL AIDS OR GEOGRAPHICAL LANDMARKS.

NEW STUDIES SHOW THAT SHAD—LARGE HERRINGS— ACHIEVE REMARKABLE MIGRATORY PRECISION BY ACCURATELY SENSING WATER TEMPERATURES.

THE AMERICAN SHAD IS THE LARGEST MEMBER OF THE HERRING FAMILY, MEASURING UP TO 20 INCHES AND WEIGHING UP TO 5 LBS.

LIKE THE SALMON, THE SHAD IS BORN IN A FRESHWATER RIVER, THEN TRAVELS DOWN TO THE SEA, WHERE IT REMAINS FOR PERHAPS SIX YEARS TO REACH MATURITY, AND FINALLY RETURNS TO ITS HOME RIVER TO SPAWN.

VAST SHOALS OF SHAD LIVE OFF THE U.S. ATLANTIC COAST, AND EACH YEAR THE ANNUAL "SHAD RUN" INTO THE RIVERS IS A DRAMATIC BIOLOGICAL AND ECONOMIC EVENT.

Maine
U.S.A.
Florida

THE SHAD ENTER RIVER AFTER RIVER TO A TIMETABLE THAT NEVER VARIES FOR MORE THAN A FEW DAYS FROM YEAR TO YEAR. SCIENTISTS HAVE LONG WONDERED WHAT CONTROLS AND DIRECTS THIS MASS MOVEMENT. . .

CIENTISTS HAVE ECENTLY STUDIED SHAD OVEMENTS BY ATTACHING ONAR TRANSMITTERS TO HEIR BACKS, AS WELL S BY TAGGING THEM.

USA.
spawning rivers

ST. JOHNS R.

SAVANNAH R.

YORK R.

SUSQUEHANNA R.

HUDSON R.

CONNECTICUT R.

ST. LAWRENCE R.

Great Lakes

S ← → North

CANADA

ST. JOHN R.

February

January March

December

April

November

May

October

June

July, August, September

ANNUAL MOVEMENT OF SHAD

THEY NOW KNOW THAT THE ADULT SHAD FOLLOW A REMARKABLY REGULAR ROUTE AND TIMETABLE FROM THE SUMMER GATHERING GROUNDS IN THE GULF OF MAINE TO THEIR HOME RIVERS WHERE THEY WERE BORN AND WHERE THEY WILL SPAWN.

THEY ALSO DISCOVERED THAT SHAD MOVE IN ORDER TO REMAIN WITHIN A VERY NARROW TEMPERATURE RANGE IN BOTH OCEAN AND RIVERS.

CIENTISTS INVESTIGATING HAD MIGRATION FOUND HAT THE FISH MOVED IN RDER TO REMAIN IN ATER BETWEEN 13 DEG.C ND 19 DEG. C.

Newfoundland

SPRING

movement of shad

AUTUMN

Florida

TO STAY WITHIN THIS RANGE THE SHOALS MOVE NORTH IN SPRING AND SOUTH IN AUTUMN, AS THE COASTAL WATER TEMPERATURES CHANGE WITH SEASONS.

THIS MOVEMENT ALSO BRINGS THEM TO THEIR HOME RIVERS AT THE TIME WHEN THE WATER TEMPERATURE IN THE STREAMS IS OPTIMAL FOR SPAWNING AND EGG HATCHING — 15 DEG. C TO 26 DEG. C.

general movement of shad

WHAT REMAINS UNEXPLAINED IS HOW THE SHAD SWIMMING UP THE COAST KNOW THAT THEY HAVE REACHED THE PARTICULAR RIVER IN WHICH THEY WERE BORN.

XPERIMENTS IN WHICH SHAD AD THEIR SENSE OF MELL BLOCKED SUGGEST HAT THEY ACTUALLY ENTIFY THE RIVER IN HICH THEY WERE BORN Y DETECTING CHEMICAL UBSTANCES HARACTERISTIC OF THAT VER ALONE.

RIVER

course followed by fish

SEA

WHEN LEAVING THE SEA FOR FRESH WATER, SHAD WILL MEANDER BETWEEN THE TWO FOR A FEW DAYS TO ADJUST THEIR SYSTEM TO THE CHANGE IN SALINITY, WHICH IF MADE ABRUPTLY MIGHT KILL THEM.

SHAD CAN ALSO DETECT NETS ACROSS THE RIVERS, EVEN IN TOTAL DARKNESS, AND THEY OFTEN TURN ASIDE.

THUS ALTHOUGH THE INGENIOUS TEMPERATURE-SENSING ABILITIES OF SHAD ARE BECOMING BETTER UNDERSTOOD, THERE ARE MANY MYSTERIES YET TO BE SOLVED ABOUT THEIR BEHAVIOR. . . .

Pathfinding penguin

Some of the most notable feats of navigation are made
penguins, which walk rather than fly across the Antarctic ice-ca

IN 1959, FIVE ADULT PENGUINS WERE CAPTURED AT THEIR BREEDING GROUND IN ANTARCTICA AND BANDED BY U.S. SCIENTISTS.

THESE FLIGHTLESS BIRDS WERE TAKEN TO THE OTHER SIDE OF THE ICECAP AND RELEASED NEAR McMURDO SOUND, 1,200 MILES FROM HOME.

TEN MONTHS LATER THREE OF THE FIVE PENGUINS APPEARED AT THEIR OWN NESTS, AFTER WALKING, SWIMMING, OR TOBOGGANING ACROSS THE FEATURELESS CONTINENT.

THIS EXTRAORDINARY NAVIGATIONAL FEAT IS NOW BEING STUDIED FO FURTHER CLUES TO THI AGE-OLD MYSTERY OI ANIMAL MIGRATION.

TODAY SCIENTISTS IN MANY COUNTRIES HAVE BEGUN TO UNRAVEL THE MYSTERY OF 'NATURE'S "COMPASS" IN MIGRATING BIRDS, ANIMALS, AND EVEN FISH.

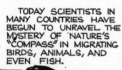

FOLLOWING WORK IN GERMANY, IT IS NOW CLEAR THAT MANY BIRDS ORIENTATE THEM-SELVES BY THE SUN.

BUT EVEN WITH TINY RADIO TRANSMITTERS FITTED TO BIRDS, SCIENTISTS HAVE LITTLE KNOWLEDGE OF THEIR MOVEMENTS ONCE RELEASED.

THIS PROBLEM FINALLY S TWO U.S. ZOOLOGISTS TO THE SOUTH POLE TO STUD MIGRATING PENGUINS, WHIC WALK

ANTARCTIC PENGUINS ...PEND THE WINTER ON THE ...TER FRINGE OF THE ...CK ICE, FISHING IN THE ...EN SEA.

EACH SPRING, HOWEVER, THEY TRAVEL HUNDREDS OF MILES TO THEIR ROOKERIES ON THE ROCKY MAINLAND TO BREED, ALWAYS IN THE SAME PLACE.

HOW THEY NAVIGATE IN AN AREA WITHOUT RECOGNIZABLE LANDMARKS REMAINS ONE OF NATURE'S GREAT MYSTERIES.

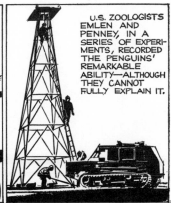

U.S. ZOOLOGISTS EMLEN AND PENNEY, IN A SERIES OF EXPERIMENTS, RECORDED THE PENGUINS' REMARKABLE ABILITY—ALTHOUGH THEY CANNOT FULLY EXPLAIN IT.

PENGUINS TAKEN ...UNDREDS OF MILES ...ROM HOME WERE ...LACED ONE AT A TIME ...I A COVERED PIT IN A ...LAT, FEATURELESS ...ANDSCAPE.

WHEN RELEASED, THEIR POSITION WAS PLOTTED EVERY FIVE MINUTES FROM THREE OBSERV-ATION TOWERS.

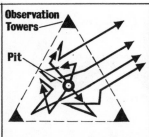

Observation Towers

Pit

NEARLY ALL PENGUINS, AFTER INITIAL RANDOM MOVEMENTS, HEADED OFF IN A STRAIGHT LINE IN THE SAME DIRECTION UNTIL OUT OF SIGHT.

WHEN THE SUN WAS OB-SCURED BY CLOUDS, HOWEVER, THE BIRDS WENT OFF IN ALL DIRECTIONS. BUT THIS "SUN COMPASS" IS OVERSHADOWED BY AN EVEN MORE REMARKABLE MECHANISM.

RELEASED IN STRANGE ...OUNTRY IN THE MORNING, ...LL PENGUINS HEADED UN-...RRINGLY NORTHWARDS, WITH ...HE SUN TO THEIR RIGHT.

TWELVE HOURS LATER, WITH THE ANTARCTIC SUMMER SUN (WHICH NEVER SETS) NOW ON THEIR LEFT, THEY WERE STILL HEAD-ING DUE NORTH.

TO ALLOW FOR THE MOVEMENT OF A SUN WHICH TRAVELS SIDEWAYS AND NOT OVERHEAD, PENGUINS MUST HAVE A "BIOLOGICAL CLOCK" WHICH CORRECTS THEIR SUN COMPASS.

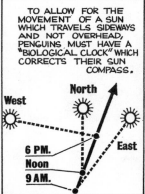

West   North   East

6 PM.
Noon
9 AM.

THIS NORTH – FINDING ABILITY, HOWEVER, STILL DOES NOT EXPLAIN HOW PENGUINS FIND THEIR WAY HOME, WHICH MAY BE IN A COMPLETELY DIFFERENT DIRECTION . . .

Home without a ma[p]

Penguins can find their home rookery, no matter where they [are] released in Antarctica, despite the lack of topographical feat[ures] which might provide "map references".

A MAN, SET DOWN IN A STRANGE COUNTRY WITH A COMPASS, CAN FIND HIS WAY TO A DISTANT POINT....

... BUT ONLY IF HE HAS A MAP SHOWING WHERE HE IS AND WHERE HE WANTS TO GET TO.

THE ANTARCTIC PENGUIN CAN FIND ITS WAY HOME ACROSS UNKNOWN COUNTRY WITHOUT A MAP —— AND WITHOUT THE TOPOGRAPHICAL INFORMATION AVAILABLE TO A FLYING BIRD.

SCIENTISTS ARE SEEKING CLUES IN THE PENGUIN'S HABIT OF ALWAYS HEADING NORTH WHEN RELEASED FROM CAPTIVITY.

U.S. SCIENTISTS TOOK PENGUINS FROM ONE OF THE MAIN ANTARCTIC ROOKERIES, AT CAPE CROZIER.

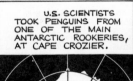

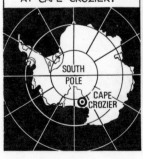

RELEASED AT FIVE DIFFERENT POINTS, THEY ALL HEADED ALONG COURSES PARALLEL TO A LINE RUNNING NORTH —NORTHEAST THROUGH THEIR HOME ROOKERY.

PENGUINS BROUGHT FROM THE RUSSIAN BASE AT MIRNY TOOK A DIFFERENT DIRECTION—— BUT PARALLEL TO A SIMILAR NORTH—NORTHEAST LINE THROUGH MIRNY.

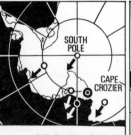

THUS ALL PENGUINS ESCAPING FROM CAPTIVITY HEADED ALMOST DIRECTLY AWAY FROM THE SOUTH POLE, OR TOWARDS THE EDGE OF THE CONTINENT.

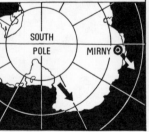

THE FACT THAT ALL PENGUINS RELEASED IN STRANGE COUNTRY HEADED NORTHWARDS SHOWS THAT THEIR "COMPASS" IS NOTHING TO DO WITH THEIR SURROUNDINGS...

...BUT IS IN FACT AN OBJECT 93,000,000 MILES AWAY —— THE SUN.

SOME IN-BUILT BIOLOGICAL "CLOCK" ENABLES THEM TO CALCULATE, FROM THE SUN'S POSITION AT A CERTAIN TIME, WHERE NORTH LIES.

THE REASON THEY ALL HEAD NORTH, HOWEVER, AND NOT IN ANY OTHER DIRECTION, STILL PUZZLES SCIENTISTS.

RELEASED PENGUINS PROBABLY ESCAPE NORTH BECAUSE THIS COURSE WOULD LEAD THEM FROM THEIR HOME ROOKERY TO THE SEA.

THE SEA, THEIR ONLY SOURCE OF FOOD, THEREFORE REPRESENTS SURVIVAL.

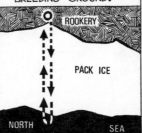

IN SPRING, SOME INSTINCTIVE SIGNAL WHICH TURNED THEM PRECISELY 180 DEGREES AWAY FROM NORTH WOULD THEN LEAD THEM BACK TO THEIR BREEDING GROUND.

ROOKERY
PACK ICE
NORTH   SEA

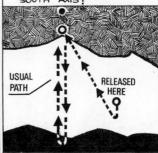

BUT HOW DO THEY FIND THE ROOKERY EVEN WHEN DISPLACED THOUSANDS OF MILES FROM THIS NORTH-SOUTH AXIS?

USUAL PATH
RELEASED HERE

PENGUINS RELEASED AWAY FROM THEIR ROOKERY ALWAYS HEAD NORTH, EVEN THOUGH THIS MAY BE AWAY FROM HOME TO BEGIN WITH.

WHAT NEW INFORMATION DO THE BIRDS RECEIVE DURING THEIR TRAVELS WHICH ENABLES THEM TO CORRECT COURSE AND RETURN HOME, WITH NO LANDMARKS?

SOUTH POLE   MIRNY

CAPE CROZIER

THIS ABILITY, WHICH SCIENCE CANNOT YET EXPLAIN, IS ONE OF THE GREAT PUZZLES OF THE ANIMAL KINGDOM.

THUS MAN REMAINS FAR FROM UNDERSTANDING, LET ALONE SURPASSING, ALL THE WORKINGS OF THE NATURAL WORLD...

The complexities of slee

For the brain, sleep is far removed from the state of rest
relaxation that overtakes the body.

ONE OF THE STRANGEST BEHAVIORAL HABITS OF ANIMALS IS SLEEP. ITS PRECISE FUNCTION IS STILL NOT FULLY UNDERSTOOD.

SLEEP MAY BE UTILIZED BY THE BODY TO RESTORE TIRED MUSCLES— BUT DURING SLEEP THE BRAIN IS NOT RESTING.

IN FACT, DURING SOME PHASES OF SLEEP THE BRAIN IS MORE ACTIVE THAN DURING WAKEFULNESS—— THE INTERLUDES CALLED "PARADOXICAL" SLEEP.

RECENT RESEARCH SUGGE THAT "PARADOXICAL" SLE IS ACTUALLY USED FOR BRAIN GROWTH AND RENEWAL. . . .

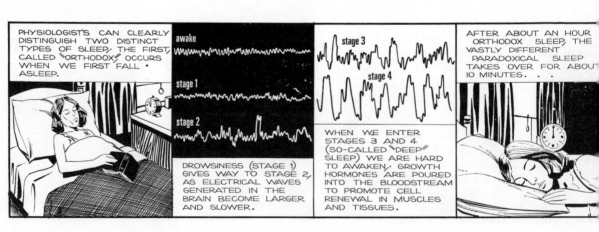

PHYSIOLOGISTS CAN CLEARLY DISTINGUISH TWO DISTINCT TYPES OF SLEEP. THE FIRST, CALLED "ORTHODOX" OCCURS WHEN WE FIRST FALL ASLEEP.

awake

stage 1

stage 2

DROWSINESS (STAGE 1) GIVES WAY TO STAGE 2, AS ELECTRICAL WAVES GENERATED IN THE BRAIN BECOME LARGER AND SLOWER.

stage 3

stage 4

WHEN WE ENTER STAGES 3 AND 4 (SO-CALLED "DEEP" SLEEP) WE ARE HARD TO AWAKEN. GROWTH HORMONES ARE POURED INTO THE BLOODSTREAM TO PROMOTE CELL RENEWAL IN MUSCLES AND TISSUES.

AFTER ABOUT AN HOUR ORTHODOX SLEEP, THE VASTLY DIFFERENT PARADOXICAL SLEEP TAKES OVER FOR ABOUT 10 MINUTES. . . .

PARADOXICAL SLEEP WITH ITS HIGH BRAIN ACTIVITY ALTERNATES WITH AN HOUR OF DEEP ORTHODOX SLEEP ABOUT FIVE TIMES A NIGHT.

...RING THE 10 MINUTE ...RIODS OF PARADOXICAL ...EEP THE EYES MAKE ...PID MOVEMENTS, AND ...LSE AND BREATHING RATES ...LE IRREGULAR. DREAMS ...CUR ONLY DURING THESE PERIODS.

IF WE ARE AWAKENED AFTER PARADOXICAL SLEEP, DREAMS ARE OFTEN VIVIDLY CLEAR. IF AFTER ORTHODOX SLEEP, THERE MAY BE NO MEMORY OF DREAMING AT ALL.

RECENT RESEARCH AT EDINBURGH UNIVERSITY HAS PROVIDED NEW MEANING FOR THIS STRANGE, MENTALLY RESTLESS TYPE OF SLEEP...

THEY NOTED A BLOOD FLOW THROUGH THE BRAIN FAR ABOVE WAKING LEVELS, APPARENTLY TO REMOVE EXCESS HEAT PRODUCED BY THE EXTRA ACTIVITY.

...SEARCHERS ...UGHT AN ...PLANATION FOR THE ...TENSE ACTIVITY IN ...E BRAIN'S LIVING ...EMISTRY DURING ...ARADOXICAL SLEEP.

WHILE BRAIN CELLS THEMSELVES ARE NOT RENEWED, LIKE OTHER BODY CELLS, THEIR PROTEIN CONSTITUENTS NEED CONSTANT REPLACEMENT.

EXPERIMENTS NOW SHOW THAT WHEN THE BRAIN IS FORCED INTO EXTRA RENEWAL ACTIVITY, THERE IS A GREAT INCREASE IN PARADOXICAL SLEEP...

...BURGH DOCTORS TOOK DRUGS WHICH CAUSE ...D CHEMICAL DAMAGE TO THE BRAIN, AND ALSO ...DUCE THE PROPORTION OF PARADOXICAL ...EEP. THE SUBSEQUENT BIG INCREASE COINCIDED ...TH THE BRAIN'S REPLACEMENT OF DRUG-DAMAGED ...L PROTEINS.

'Rebound' increase of paradoxical sleep

Injections of heroin for a week

2 MONTHS

Normal proportion of paradoxical sleep

A SIMILAR INCREASE IN PARADOXICAL SLEEP ACCOMPANIES BRAIN RECOVERY FROM MANY KINDS OF CHEMICAL, ELECTRICAL, MECHANICAL, OR PSYCHOLOGICAL DAMAGE.

THUS THAT 10 MINUTE PHASE OF MENTALLY RESTLESS, PARADOXICAL SLEEP ABOUT EVERY HOUR DURING THE NIGHT IS VITAL TO THE EFFICIENCY OF OUR MOST VITAL ORGAN, THE BRAIN...

The diving refle.

One of the most interesting vestiges of man's evolution f
sea-dwelling animals is the persistence of a powerful reaction to
immersion of the face in water.

EACH YEAR TENS OF THOUSANDS OF BABIES ARE FOUND DEAD IN THEIR CRIBS, WITHOUT ANY PHYSICAL SIGN OF ILLNESS OR INJURY.

OCCASIONALLY GOOD SWIMMERS DROWN FOR NO APPARENT REASON, AND THE BLAME IS PLACED ON "CRAMP".

SOMETIMES A SUSPECTED CORONARY VICTIM TURNS OUT TO HAVE NO BLOCKED ARTERIES TO ACCOUNT FOR HIS CONDITION.

REMARKABLY ENOUGH, RECENT RESEARCH WITH SEALS SUGGESTS THAT ALL THESE MYSTERIOUS DEATHS MIGHT BE LINKE THROUGH AN EVOLUTIONA MECHANISM WHICH STILL PERSISTS IN MAN —— T DIVING REFLEX.

THE ABILITY OF SOME AIR-BREATHING MAMMALS SUCH AS SEALS AND WALRUSES TO STAY UNDER WATER UP TO HALF AN HOUR HAS LONG PUZZLED BIOLOGISTS.

MOST CREATURES, INCLUDING MAN, BLACK OUT AND DIE WITHIN A FEW MINUTES, THROUGH OXYGEN STARVATION OF THE BRAIN.

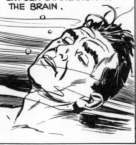

RECENTLY, SCIENTISTS AT THE SCRIPPS INSTITUTION OF OCEANOGRAPHY IN CALIFORNIA HAVE GONE A LONG WAY TOWARDS EXPLAINING BOTH SETS OF PHENOMENA.

THEY BEGAN THEIR EXPERI- MENTS BY CATCHING ELEPHA SEALS, WEIGHING UP TO 2,(LBS, WHICH ARE AMONG LARGEST SEA-GOING MAMM

TO STUDY THEIR SEAL, SCIENTISTS ATTACHED INSTRUMENTS TO VARIOUS PARTS OF ITS BODY, INCLUDING THE ARTERIES IN ITS FLIPPERS.

WHEN IT WAS LOWERED INTO WATER IN A SLING, IMMEDIATE AND STRIKING PHYSIOLOGICAL ADJUST— MENTS TOOK PLACE.

AS SOON AS ITS NOSE WENT UNDER, THE SEAL'S HEART BEAT DROPPED FROM 80 PER MINUTE TO 12 — WHICH WOULD CON— SERVE THE OXYGEN ALREADY IN THE BLOODSTREAM.

FURTHERMORE, THE BLOOD VESSELS IN THE TAIL AND FLIPPERS VIRTUALLY SHUT DOWN, DIVERTING THE BODY'S OXYGEN STORE TO THE ANIMAL'S BRAIN.

A SUBMERGED SEAL ALSO OBTAINS ENERGY BY BREAKING DOWN BLOOD SUGARS WITHOUT USING ANY OF ITS LIMITED OXYGEN STORE.

SIGNS OF THIS METABOLIC CHANGE ARE INCREASED AMOUNTS OF LACTIC ACID AND POTASSIUM IN THE BLOOD.

STRANGELY ENOUGH, ALTHOUGH MAN IS FAR UP THE EVOLUTIONARY LADDER, HE STILL EXHIBITS ALL THE SIGNS OF THE DIVING REFLEX —— LOWERED HEARTBEAT, CONSTRICTED BLOOD VESSELS, METABOLIC CHANGES IN THE BLOOD!

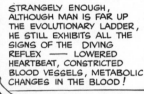

EXPERIMENTS IN CALIFORNIA WITH JAPANESE PEARL DIVERS INDICATE, IN FACT, A LINK BETWEEN THE DIVING REFLEX AND SOME HEART FAILURES ...

TESTS SHOW THAT WHEN A MAN DIPS HIS FACE IN WATER, HIS PULSE RATE MAY HALVE, AND THE ACIDITY OF HIS BLOOD INCREASES PERHAPS FOUR TIMES.

SUCH SYMPTOMS MAY ALSO CAUSE A DEADLY HEART DISTURBANCE CALLED VENTRICULAR FIBRILLATION —— AND DIVING REFLEX OUT OF CONTROL COULD KILL AN EXPERIENCED SWIMMER.

THE DIVING REFLEX CAN ALSO BE TRIGGERED WITHOUT CONTACT WITH WATER, BUT BY ANXIETY —— AND COULD CAUSE CARDIAC FAILURE WITHOUT APPARENT REASON.

A BABY ROLLING ITS FACE INTO ITS PILLOW MIGHT SET OFF A FATAL DIVING REFLEX IN AN EFFORT TO CONSERVE OXYGEN — ANOTHER REMINDER OF MAN'S LONG EVOLUTIONARY EMERGENCE FROM THE SEA ....

Angles of visio.

Recent research shows that even such a basic physical func
as the way we see can be influenced by external factors during e
development.

THE MYSTERIES OF VISION, AND THE WAY IN WHICH WE SEE THINGS, CONTINUE TO BE AN IMPORTANT ASPECT OF BEHAVIOURAL RESEARCH.

ONE DISCOVERY HAS BEEN THAT EARLY IMPRESSIONS AFTER BIRTH CAN HAVE A SIGNIFICANT EFFECT ON THE BRAIN'S ABILITY TO PERCEIVE PARTICULAR PATTERNS.

EXPERIMENTS WITH KITTENS WHICH ARE CONFINED TO A PARTICULAR ENVIRONMENT FROM BIRTH SHOW THAT THEY NEVER LEARN TO SEE CERTAIN OTHER FEATURES.

INVESTIGATIONS INTO THIS PHENOMENON IN MAN NOW SUGGE THAT OUR SEEIN ABILITY MAY ALS BE RADICALLY INFLUENCED IN THIS WAY. . .

A MILESTONE EXPERIMENT IN VISION RESEARCH WAS THE DISCOVERY THAT NERVE CELLS IN THE BRAIN OF ANIMALS LEARN TO DETECT LINES VERY SOON AFTER BIRTH.

NEWBORN KITTENS WERE KEPT IN A BOX IN WHICH, WHEN THEIR EYES OPENED, THE ONLY LINES THEY COULD SEE WERE VERTICAL.

AFTER SOME WEEKS THEY WERE RETURNED TO A NORMAL ENVIRONMENT, AND THEIR VISION TESTED AGAINST LINES OF VARYING ORIENTATION.

IT WAS FOUND THAT THEY SIMPLY DID NOT SEE HORIZONTAL LINE AT ALL, AND KEPT BUMPING INTO BARS, THE BRAIN CELL DETECTORS OF HORIZONTAL LINES HAD NOT DEVELOPED.

TENS WHICH ARE
[ORIEN]TED TO VERTICAL
[LIN]ES FROM BIRTH CANNOT
[SEE] HORIZONTAL LINES.
[IS] HUMAN VISION EQUALLY
[SUS]CEPTIBLE TO
[EAR]LY INFLUENCES?

MOST PEOPLE'S VISION
IS MUCH MORE ACUTE
FOR VERTICAL OR
HORIZONTAL LINES
THAN FOR THOSE AT
45 DEGREES LEFT
OR RIGHT.

RESEARCHERS HAVE
NOT TRIED TO
PRODUCE A SIMILAR
TOTAL "BLINDNESS" TO
LINES OF ANY GIVEN
ORIENTATION, BUT
THEY MAY NOW BE
ABLE TO EXPLAIN
ANOMALIES IN HUMAN
PERCEPTION OF LINES.

IS THIS BECAUSE
MOST PEOPLE ARE
BROUGHT UP TODAY
IN THE VERTICAL-AND-
HORIZONTAL FRAME-
WORK OF CITIES?
THERE IS SOME
EVIDENCE THAT
THIS MAY BE SO. . .

[T]WO CANADIAN
[R]ESEARCHERS DECIDED
[TO] SEE WHETHER OUR
[GE]NERALLY LESSER
[PE]RCEPTION OF
[DIA]GONAL LINES IS DUE
[TO] OUR GROWING UP IN
[TH]E VERTICAL-AND-
[HO]RIZONTAL WORLD
[OF] CITIES.

THE INDIANS COMPARED
FAVOURABLY IN
GENERAL SPATIO-
CONCEPTUAL ABILITY
WITH EUROPEAN
CANADIANS, AND IN
THE LINE TESTS DID
EVEN BETTER.

THEY SHOWED EQUALLY
HIGH PERCEPTION OF LINES
IN ALL ORIENTATIONS,
THUS SUPPORTING THE
THEORY THAT THE
SENSORY PERCEPTORS OF
OUR BRAIN MAY BE
PREJUDICED BY EARLY
EXPERIENCE.

THEY TESTED 16 CREE
INDIANS WHO STILL
LIVE IN TEPEES ON A
REMOTE COASTLINE,
WHERE THERE ARE
HARDLY ANY
STRAIGHT VERTICAL
OR HORIZONTAL LINES.

[FU]RTHER EXPERIMENTS
[R]EINFORCE THE EARLY
[FI]NDINGS THAT WHEN THE
[B]RAIN IS ORIENTATED TO
[V]ERTICALS FROM BIRTH IT
[C]ANNOT SEE HORIZONTALS.

LATER TESTS ON THE
VISION PERCEPTION
CELLS IN THE BRAIN
SHOWED THAT THEY
REACTED TO MOVING
DOTS BETTER THAN
LINES OF ANY KIND—
A CHARACTERISTIC OF
FROG VISION WHICH
HELPS IT CATCH
INSECTS.

KITTENS WERE KEPT
AFTER BIRTH IN A
DARKENED DOME
IN WHICH ALL
THEY SAW WERE
SPOTS OF LIGHT,
AS IN A PLANET-
ARIUM.

SUCH RESEARCH MAY
HELP TO EXPLAIN
THE MANY ANOMALIES
OF HUMAN VISION,
ONCE CONSIDERED
NORMAL, IN WHICH
PEOPLE "JUST DIDN'T
SEE IT. . . ."

Mind over matte

The behavior of even such involuntary functions as heart-
and blood pressure can be affected by conscious effort.

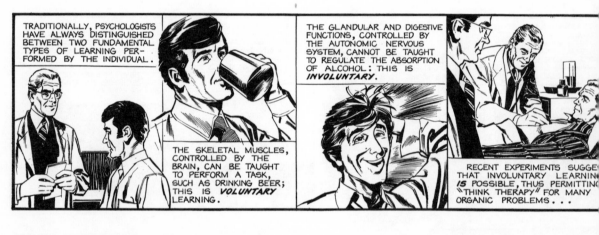

TRADITIONALLY, PSYCHOLOGISTS HAVE ALWAYS DISTINGUISHED BETWEEN TWO FUNDAMENTAL TYPES OF LEARNING PERFORMED BY THE INDIVIDUAL.

THE SKELETAL MUSCLES, CONTROLLED BY THE BRAIN, CAN BE TAUGHT TO PERFORM A TASK, SUCH AS DRINKING BEER; THIS IS *VOLUNTARY* LEARNING.

THE GLANDULAR AND DIGESTIVE FUNCTIONS, CONTROLLED BY THE AUTONOMIC NERVOUS SYSTEM, CANNOT BE TAUGHT TO REGULATE THE ABSORPTION OF ALCOHOL: THIS IS *INVOLUNTARY*.

RECENT EXPERIMENTS SUGGE THAT INVOLUNTARY LEARNIN *IS* POSSIBLE, THUS PERMITTIN "THINK THERAPY" FOR MANY ORGANIC PROBLEMS...

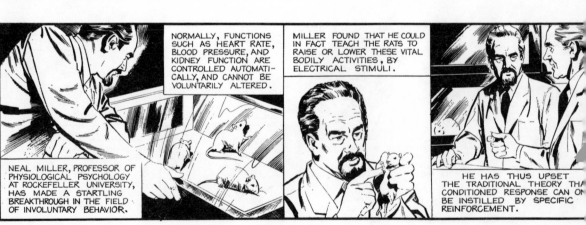

NORMALLY, FUNCTIONS SUCH AS HEART RATE, BLOOD PRESSURE, AND KIDNEY FUNCTION ARE CONTROLLED AUTOMATICALLY, AND CANNOT BE VOLUNTARILY ALTERED.

NEAL MILLER, PROFESSOR OF PHYSIOLOGICAL PSYCHOLOGY AT ROCKEFELLER UNIVERSITY, HAS MADE A STARTLING BREAKTHROUGH IN THE FIELD OF INVOLUNTARY BEHAVIOR.

MILLER FOUND THAT HE COULD IN FACT TEACH THE RATS TO RAISE OR LOWER THESE VITAL BODILY ACTIVITIES, BY ELECTRICAL STIMULI.

HE HAS THUS UPSET THE TRADITIONAL THEORY THA CONDITIONED RESPONSE CAN ON BE INSTILLED BY SPECIFIC REINFORCEMENT.

PROFESSOR MILLER AT ROCKEFELLER UNIVERSITY USED A NON-SPECIFIC REINFORCEMENT WITH RATS: A MILD STIMULATION OF THE REWARD CENTER OF THE BRAIN.

BY REWARDING THE RAT WHENEVER ITS BLOOD PRESSURE ALTERED IN THE DESIRED WAY, MILLER EVENTUALLY REVERSED THE ORDER. WHEN REWARDED, THE RAT ALTERED ITS OWN BLOOD PRESSURE.

CLASSICAL CONDITIONING [THE]ORY SAYS THAT THE [AUT]ONOMIC NERVOUS SYSTEM [CAN] BE PARTLY TRAINED BY [SPE]CIFIC REINFORCEMENT.

THUS PAVLOV'S DOGS LEARN TO SALIVATE AT THE SOUND OF A BELL— BUT ONLY AFTER FOOD HAS BECOME ASSOCIATED WITH THE SOUND OF A BELL.

[TH]E MOST INTERESTING EXAMPLE [OF] INVOLUNTARY LEARNING [CO]MES FROM AN EXPERIMENT [WIT]H MALE STUDENTS AT [HAR]VARD MEDICAL SCHOOL.

THEIR BLOOD PRESSURE— AN "UNCONSCIOUS" FUNCTION— WAS CONTINUALLY MONITORED; EACH TIME THE PRESSURE FELL, THEY WERE "REWARDED" WITH A NUDE SLIDE!

THEY WERE NOT TOLD WHAT BODILY FUNCTION THEY WERE TRYING TO MODIFY— ONLY TO TRY TO MAKE THE REWARD PICTURES APPEAR AS OFTEN AS THEY COULD.

BEFORE LONG, THEY LEARNED TO MODIFY THEIR BLOOD PRESSURE, SOMETHING WHICH ACCORDING TO TRADITIONAL PHYSIOLOGICAL THEORY IS UNTEACHABLE.

[THE] GREAT SIGNIFICANCE OF [VO]LUNTARY LEARNING [EXP]ERIMENTS IS IN THE FIELD [OF P]SYCHOSOMATIC ILLNESS: [P]HYSICAL SYMPTOMS OF [M]ENTAL MALFUNCTION.

MANAGING DIRECTOR

ILLNESS SUCH AS UPSET STOMACH BEFORE AN IMPORTANT INTERVIEW MAY HAVE BEEN UNCONSCIOUSLY "LEARNED" IN CHILDHOOD.

MOTHER MIGHT HAVE REWARDED THE CHILD BY ALLOWING IT TO STAY HOME FROM SCHOOL EXAMS, BECAUSE IT WAS ILL.

IT SHOULD THUS BE POSSIBLE TO "UNLEARN" SUCH PATTERNS— AND ALSO TO CONSCIOUSLY CONTROL ORGANIC MALFUNCTIONS NOW CONSIDERED UNCONSCIOUS ...

The power of illusio.

Some famous optical illusions illustrate the still little underst
ways in which the brain interprets data presented to it.

IT IS DIFFICULT TO BELIEVE THAT THE HORIZONTAL LINES IN THIS DIAGRAM ARE PARALLEL. OPTICAL ILLUSIONS SUCH AS THIS HAVE BEEN KNOWN FOR A LONG TIME.

EQUALLY THE OBLIQUE LINE IN THE DRAWING BELOW DOES NOT APPEAR TO BE ONE STRAIGHT LINE.

SOME SUCH ILLUSIONS WERE KNOWN TO THE ANCIENT GREEKS, BUT NO EXPERIMENTAL STUDY WAS MADE OF THEM UNTIL THE LAST HUNDRED YEARS OR SO.

IN RECENT YEARS VISUAL ILLUSIONS HAVE BEEN TH SUBJECT OF INTENSIVE ST THEY COULD YIELD IMPOR CLUES TO UNDERSTANDING HOW WE INTERPRET WHAT WE SEE.

ONE OF THE FIRST FIGURES STUDIED WAS THE "NECKER CUBE." SOMETIMES ONE FACE OF THE DIAGRAM APPEARS TO BE IN FRONT AND SOMETIMES THE OTHER.

IN A MODERN VERSION OF THIS ILLUSION THE FLY AT TIMES APPEARS INSIDE THE CAGE, AT OTHER TIMES OUTSIDE.

SUCH ILLUSIONS CONCERN IMAGES OF EQUAL OR NEARLY EQUAL PROBABILITY. THE MIND FLUCTUATES, UNABLE TO DETERMINE WHICH IS RIGHT AS IN THE CLASSIC "PROFILE-VASE" DIAGRAM.

IS THIS A VASE OR TWO FACES?

IN THE SAME WAY IT OF TAKES THE MIND SOMI TIME TO DETERMINE W THE BLACK SHAPES BE REPRESENT.

E SO-CALLED "RAILWAY LINES" USION HAS BEEN USED ENTLY IN EXPERIMENTAL RK. ALTHOUGH THE HORIZONTAL ES ARE EQUAL IN LENGTH, EY DO NOT APPEAR TO BE SO.

R.L. GREGORY OF THE UNIVERSITY OF EDINBURGH HAS SUGGESTED THAT SUCH ILLUSIONS ARISE FROM MECHANISMS THAT UNDER NORMAL CIRCUMSTANCES MAKE THE VISIBLE WORLD EASIER TO COMPREHEND.

GREGORY'S EXPLANATION OF THE "RAILWAY LINES" ILLUSION DEPENDS ON THE FACT THAT WE KNOW THAT ALTHOUGH THE MORE DISTANT RAILWAY SLEEPERS APPEAR SMALLER, THEY ARE ACTUALLY THE SAME SIZE.

THUS THE UPPER RECTANGLE IS INTERPRETED AS BEING FURTHER AWAY AND THEREFORE "MUST BE" LARGER THAN THE LOWER.

OTHER ILLUSION WHICH DR. GREGORY EDINBURGH EXPLAINS IN A SIMILAR NNER IS THE FAMOUS "ARROWHEAD USION" IN WHICH THE TWO COLUMNS PEAR TO DIFFER IN LENGTH.

HE SUGGESTS THAT THE EYE INTERPRETS THE SHORTER LINE AS THE OUTSIDE CORNER OF A BUILDING, THE EYE SHRINKING THE LENGTH TO COMPENSATE FOR PERSPECTIVE DISTORTION.

IN THE SAME WAY THE LONGER LINE IS INTERPRETED AS THE INSIDE CORNER OF A WALL AND IS ACCOMPANIED BY COMPENSATING LENGTHENING.

RECENT DISCOVERY OF ECIDABLE FIGURES" PROVIDES ENCE THAT MOST ILLUSIONS E CAUSED BY THE WAY WHICH THE BRAIN ERPRETS DATA.

THE "PRONGED BLIVET" AND THE MONUMENT BEFUDDLE THE BRAIN WITH THEIR IMPOSSIBLE STRUCTURE.

IN THE SAME CATEGORY IS THE "PENROSE STAIRCASE" WHICH GOES UP AND UP, YET ENDS WHERE IT STARTED.

ALTHOUGH THESE AND OTHER VISUAL ILLUSIONS ARE OFTEN REGARDED AS MERELY AMUSING TRICKS, THEIR STUDY IS HELPING IN FURTHERING AN UNDERSTANDING OF HOW THE BRAIN INTERPRETS DATA.

Index . . .

59-402